The Aes Coinage of Emporion

Leandre Villaronga

translated from the Spanish by
Elisabeth Weeks

BAR Supplementary Series 23
1977

British Archaeological Reports

122, Banbury Road, Oxford OX2 7BP, England

GENERAL EDITORS

A. C. C. Brodribb, M.A. A. R. Hands, B.Sc., M.A., D.Phil.
Mrs. Y. M. Hands D. R. Walker, M.A.

<u>B.A.R.</u> Supplementary Series 23, 1977: "The Aes Coinage of Emporion"
© Leandre Villaronga, 1977

The author's moral rights under the 1988 UK Copyright,
Designs and Patents Act are hereby expressly asserted.

All rights reserved. No part of this work may be copied, reproduced, stored,
sold, distributed, scanned, saved in any form of digital format or transmitted
in any form digitally, without the written permission of the Publisher.

ISBN 9780904531701 paperback
ISBN 9781407339740 e-book
DOI https://doi.org/10.30861/9780904531701
A catalogue record for this book is available from the British Library
This book is available at www.barpublishing.com

CONTENTS

	Page
Preface	
Abbreviations	
Historical Background	1
Silver Coinage	2
The Literature	4
Inscriptions	5
Foundation of the <u>Municipium</u> of Emporia	6
Typology	6
Symbols	8
Epigraphy	9
Value Marks	10
Graffito	11
Magistrates	12
Countermarks	16
Weight standards/Metrology	17
Finds of coins	22
Classification Criteria	24
Chronology	28
Catalogue	32
Note on use of the catalogue	32
Table of Iberian inscriptions with transcription	35
Key to catalogue	37
Catalogue	42
Plates	85

PREFACE

After publishing some preliminary work on the subject of the present monograph, we are returning to this topic with a larger body of material, which has enabled us to reach firmer conclusions on certain points, although in general, the results obtained are not as definitive as we should have liked. However, we are glad to be able to provide a catalogue of 2000 coins, and a full account of the problems encountered in the numismatics of Emporion.

We wish to thank all the museums, their directors and curators, and all the collectors who appear in the catalogue, for their valuable assistance, without which the present work would not have been possible.

ABBREVIATIONS

CRAWF.	M. H. Crawford, <u>Roman Republican Coinage</u>, Cambridge 1974.
E L H	<u>Enciclopedia Lingüistica Hispana</u>, Madrid 1960.
LMPER	A. M. de Guadan, <u>Las monedas de plata de Emporion y Rhode</u>, Barcelona 1968-70.
RIC	H. Mattingly and E. A. Sydenham, <u>Roman Imperial Coinage</u>, London 1923ff.
MLH	J. Untermann, <u>Monumenta Linguarum Hispanicarum</u>, Weisbaden 1975.
V.64	L. Villaronga, <u>Los magistrados en las amonedaciones latinas de Emporiae</u>, in <u>Estudios de Numismática Romana</u>, Barcelona 1964.
V.72	L. Villaronga, <u>Sistematización del bronce ibérico emporitano</u>, in <u>Acta Numismática</u> II, 1972.
V	A. Vives Escudero, <u>La Moneda Hispánica</u>, Madrid 1926.

HISTORICAL BACKGROUND

In the extreme north-east of the Iberian Peninsula and in the north-east corner of Catalonia, on a plain at the foot of Mount Canigou, which rises at the eastern end of the Pyrenees and forms a background to the Bay of Rosas, lies the site of the ancient city of Emporion, which gave this region its name, L'Empordà. It belongs to the municipality of L'Escala, in the province of Gerona, and its ruins lie between this town and Sant Martí d'Empúries.

Excavations were begun in 1908 and the finds are shared between museums in Barcelona and Gerona and a museum set up on the site.

The city was founded in 575 B.C. by Greek colonists from Phocea, in Asia Minor, who had already founded colonies at Alàlia and Messalia. The importance of Emporion in antiquity is shown by references to the city by Scylax of Carianda writing about 490 B.C., and by Skymnos, although they mention it only briefly when describing this part of the Iberian Peninsula.[1]

The friendship of the Greek colonists for the Romans led to an alliance with them against the Carthaginian invaders,[2] and Emporion was the place chosen for the Roman landing in 218 B.C.,[3] and became the first Roman military base at the start of the Second Punic War.

Livy[4] records the arrival of M. Porcius Cato at Emporion in 197 B.C., and says that the city was made up of two towns[5] separated by a wall, one inhabited by Greeks who came originally from Phocea, and the other by natives. Later, he adds, they were united in a Roman colony founded by Caesar after his victory over the sons of Pompey.

Livy gives an account of Cato's campaign of pacification, and mentions Emporion as being near his camp.[6] After the pacification of Catalonia was completed the Romans set up their base of operations at Tarraco, and the colony disappears from the literature.

The native inhabitants of the region of Emporion are referred to as indigetes by two ancient historians, Sallust[7] and Pliny.[8] Strabo[9] also mentions them, saying that Emporion was founded from Messalia, and describing the city as consisting of two towns, one inhabited by the Greek colonists and the other by the indiketai, adding that in time the two parts came to form a single city.

The final mention in the literature is by Stephen of Byzantium,[10] the geographer who lived around 500 A.D., who is the only writer to refer to indike as a city. In our opinion this is a mistake made by a writer who lived at a great distance from Emporion both in time and space.

SILVER COINAGE

The first coins to be minted in Spain were struck at Emporion, as can be seen from an examination of the hoard of coins known as the treasure of Auriol.[11] This treasure of Auriol, found near Marseilles, was hidden in about 470 B.C., and is made up of many different types of coins which are derived from Greek models, particularly from Phocea. One of them, depicting the head of a sheep, also occurs in Catalonian finds, but its style is barbaric.

From these first coins are derived others, occurring only in Catalonian hoards found at Pont de Molins, Morella and Emporion. The earliest of these coins have no inscriptions, but later they are inscribed with the letters E and M, the first letters of Emporion, and so can be attributed with certainty to this city.[12]

These small silver coins, earlier than drachmas, span the whole of the fourth century B.C., and it is only at the beginning of the third century that the first drachmas of Emporion make their appearance. These were minted[13] under the economic influence of the Carthaginians, as can be seen from the designs used, the obverse depicting Persephone, recognisable by the ear of wheat in her head-dress, like the Carthaginian Tanit-Persephone, and the reverse depicting a standing horse.[14]

Carthaginian defeat at the end of the First Punic War, in 241 B.C., brought to a close the minting of this type of drachma at Emporion. The Persephone was replaced by the Sicilian Arethusa, surrounded by three dolphins, and the standing horse was replaced by a Pegasus.

During the whole of the second half of the third century Emporion continued to mint drachmas and their fractions,[15] and towards the beginning of the Second Punic War a notable change took place in their typology, the head of the Pegasus being replaced by a small man grasping his toes, known as Kabeirus.

In 218 B.C., when the Romans landed, large numbers of drachmas were minted at Emporion, all with a Kabeirus in place of the head of the Pegasus. Their weight, which was originally 4.70 g, was reduced to 4.50 g, the same weight as the Roman denarius, which was introduced at that time.

The native Iberians, fighting first against the Carthaginians and later against the Romans, needed money to finance their wars, and minted coins in imitation of those minted at Emporion; this was the "argentum oscense" of the Roman triumphs.

The last drachmas were minted at Emporion in 195 B.C., at the time of Cato's pacification, and these have many symbols, in Roman style. However, when the weight of the Roman denarius was reduced their production ceased.

This period, the beginning of the second century B.C., saw the end of the production of silver coins at Emporion, and the introduction of bronze coins, with the Iberian inscription UNTIKESKEN,[16] which is the name of the native inhabitants of the city and its hinterland.

THE LITERATURE

The first attempt to classify the bronze coins of Emporion was made by Pujol y Camps.[17] Although simple, this first system of classification was most valuable for reference and the identification of new varieties. Later, Pujol y Camps made some improvements to his system.[18]

Shortly afterwards, Zobel[19] dealt with the coins of Emporion in a more general work, but introduced no new material.

Vives[20] was the first to attempt a complete classification of coins from Emporion, although this section is one of the weakest in his important work. He does not give a complete list of magistrates for the Latin coins.

Although his commentaries are valuable, Hill[21] adds nothing new to the material on the Iberian coinage of Emporion. As regards the Latin, he considers that there were two mints, one of which at first produced coins with the inscription MUNICI, and later coins without the names of magistrates, and the other which changed over from Iberian types to coins inscribed with names of magistrates, whereupon the first mint ceased production and the coins without names of magistrates were countermarked.

Beltran[22] thinks that the Latin coins date from 45 B.C., following on from the Iberian coins of the MUNICI type. M. Grant[23] heads the Latin issues with the MUNICI type, which he also dates from 45 B.C.

Guadan[24] gives a chronology as well as a classification, placing in period 3, from 206-133, the Iberian coins whose epigraphy has the old KE; in periods 4 and 5 (133-105 and 105-82) the coins with the later KE; and in period 6 (82-40) the coins with a Pegasus with a normal head.

Untermann[25] gives a complete bibliography up to 1971 for the Iberian coins of Emporion, but is content to follow Vives' classification, which is not sufficiently systematized. In answer to our hypothesis that some of the inscriptions on the reverses denote value, Untermann cites a semis inscribed with ETEBAN and one with EBOR although he does not know of the coins inscribed with ETAR, all of which cases will be discussed later. We are surprised to see that Untermann interprets the Latin XV as TAN.

The author of this paper has previously published separate monographs on the coins from Emporion with the Iberian inscription UNTIKESKEN,[26] and those with a Latin inscription.[27] In the present work, for which more material was available, some 2000 coins are described individually in the catalogue, and two issues are included which were absent from the original material, but were later brought to the author's notice.[28]

In addition, two important corrections were made with reference to the coins with Latin inscriptions. The first concerns the interpretation of the letter Q, which appears immediately after the names of magistrates, as QUAESTOR and not QUINQUENNALES, as previously suggested; and the second, which follows on from this, as well as from the metrological data, and from a study of the circulation of coins in Emporion, concerns a new and later chronology, since it is no longer necessary or justifiable to assume a five year period for each issue with the names of magistrates.

INSCRIPTIONS

The inscription in Iberian characters which we have no hesitation in reading as UNTIKESKEN, is an ethnic with the ending - SKEN. When Latinized it appears in the ancient texts as INDIGETES,[29] and designates the inhabitants of the city of Emporion and the surrounding area. We do not believe in the existence of the city called INDIKA, mentioned only by Stephen of Byzantium at a much later date, and the inscription on the coins is another reason for rejecting this hypothesis. In Latin indigete means "peasant", and this may have been the origin of the name, for the natives of the district of Emporion were, of course, the peasants of the Greek colony.

There is a radical change when we come to the coins with Latin inscriptions, for the name of the people in whose area the coins circulated is replaced by the name of the city which issued them.

In only one issue does the inscription MUNICI EMPORIA appear in the nominative singular; in the ancient texts it is always found in the nominative plural as EMPORIAE.

In the other Latin issues, the inscription is abbreviated in one way or another: EMPOR; the name with the M joined to the P, EMPORI or EMPORIT.

This last form, the oldest and the one that is most often used, seems to us to be either an abbreviation of EMPORITON, the Greek form transcribed in Latin script, or as Mateu Llopsis suggest, an abbreviation of EMPORITANUM,[30] used as an adjective to qualify Municipium.

The other forms may also be abbreviations of Emporiton, Emporitanum or Emporia, the latter possibly corresponding best to the most Latinized and latest issues.

THE FOUNDATION OF THE MUNICIPIUM OF EMPORIA

It has generally been supposed that the Municipium of Emporia was founded by Caesar, the authority for this being Livy, 34.9.3, in the passage where, after referring to the two cities inhabited respectively by the Greeks and Indigetes, he says "a third race was added, the Roman colonists, introduced by the divine Caesar after the defeat of Pompey's armies, and these three cities are today one. First the Hispanic people and then the Greeks became Roman citizens".

Almagro[31] believes that the foundation of a Roman colony at Emporion had a political purpose, the subjection of the city, which in his view was pro-Pompey, as was Massalia, the other Greek colony, when Caesar arrived there in 49 B.C.

Sanmarti[32] puts forward the interesting hypothesis that the colony could have been founded about 90 B.C. Grant[33] has a long section on Emporia, which he considers was one of the most important Roman towns.

As none of the ancient texts mention the Municipium when referring to Emporion, the only proof of its existence is the inscription MUNICI EMPORIA on coins of issue no. 69, which show a radical change of type, with Diana replacing Pallas. It follows that the Municipium could have been founded after Caesar established the colony.

TYPOLOGY

The typology of the coins of Emporion is fairly uniform, and only a few issues, those with a great deal of fractional currency, have different reverse types, in order to distinguish between the coins.

In general, the value of the coins is shown by the following reverse types: the Pegasus for the as, a bull for the semis, a lion for the quadrans and a horse for the sextans. In the issue with a distinctive metrological system the reverses are different.

PALLAS ATHENA. The head of Pallas Athena wearing a Corinthian helmet appears on the obverse of all the bronze coins of Emporion with Iberian inscriptions, and on all but one of those with Latin inscriptions, the odd one out depicting Diana. The type is similar to that of the denarii of the Roman Republic, but its models must be sought in Sicily and the south of Italy, especially in Syracuse,[34] Cales,[35] Luceria[36] and Teate.[37] There is also a very close model in the trientes of the series with a Roman prow.[38]

During the two centuries and more in which this type of obverse was in use there were great variations in style, corresponding to different periods and the different degrees of skill of those responsible for dies in the mint at Emporion.

The style of the first issues is very good, as they are copied directly from the models. The helmet is rounded and made all in one piece, and has a visor and a plume on top with the hair showing underneath.

The first variation is the helmet made in two sections; then, in the course of successive issues, the helmet gradually decreases in size.

DIANA. Diana appears on only one issue, in the form of a bust with bow and quiver, which was also exceptionally used in the last issues of drachmas at Emporion.[39] Diana appears on all the silver coins of Messalia,[40] and her appearance in Emporion can only be due to the veneration in which she was held by the Julian family, a veneration which Augustus showed by his dedication to her after Agrippa's victory over Sextus Pompey at Naulochus, in 36 B.C.,[41] and by the minting of coins with Diana on the reverse at Lugdunum in about 14 B.C.[42]

PEGASUS. When the bronze coinage was introduced, the reverse used was the same as had been used for the silver coinage, that is, the Pegasus with the head modified as a Kabeirus,[43] which indicated the value of one as. Towards the end of the issues with Iberian inscriptions, the Pegasus reverted to a normal head, and this is how it appears in all the issues with Latin inscriptions.

THE BULL. The bull is always used on semises and is seen charging to the right. Its closest model may have been Massalian,[44] but its origin is Sicilian.[45]

THE LION. A lion facing right appears on the reverse of the quadrans, and is also to be found in the single series no. 4, where it represents the value of one unit, although in this case it is depicted somewhat differently. In the first case the lion is erect, almost rampant, and in the second passant and sometimes with its head lowered, as if sniffing the ground. Its closest model is to be found in Massalia, where it appears on drachmas and small bronze coins.[46]

THE RUNNING HORSE. This was used on all coins with the value of a sextans, which are only found in the earliest series. We believe its origin to be Sicilian rather than Carthaginian as it appears on the coins of Timoleon of Syracuse,[47] and even on the Carthaginian coins from Sicily.[48] It was also used in the south of Italy in the first Roman issues,[49] and in Larinum, Arpi, Salapia and Thurium.[50]

THE SEA HORSE. This was used for coins with the value of half a unit in the series with a distinctive metrological system. Its origin is Sicilian and it appears on coins from Syracuse[51] and on some from Etruria.[52]

THE COCK. The cock appears on coins with the value of a quarter in series 4. It is erect with a flower in its beak. The cock without the flower was produced by some mints in southern Italy: at Caleno, Suessa and Teanum.[53] There is a Roman sextans[54] with the bird in the same position, holding a flower in its beak, but it is thought to be an eagle.

WILD BOAR. This appears on coins with the value of a sixth in the single series to which we referred above. There is an almost exactly similar representation from Arpi,[55] and it was also used in other Spanish mints, for example in Castudo.[56]

THE ALTAR AND BOARD. In a late issue which we have attributed to Emporion, some very unusual types are to be found. The obverse has a board with two "fasces" beside it and the linked letters V and L above it. The reverse has an altar with three parallel lines crossing diagonally from opposite corners, a vertical line above it, and two pellets, one on each side.[57] Perhaps this might be a curule chair which, together with the fasces, would denote a legate of Augustus.

SECONDARY TYPES

Included here are a few variations on the types already described: the addition of a laurel wreath above the Pegasus, bull or lion; and a crescent moon above the bull.

LAUREL WREATH. This symbol always carries some implication of victory, since a laurel wreath was given to the victor. Its symbolism is the same as that of the goddess Nike and although she does not appear beside the laurel wreath, it must have the same meaning. This symbol was previously used on some drachmas of Emporion.[58]

THE CRESCENT MOON. The symbol of the crescent moon comes from the east via the Phoenicians and is very common on Spanish coins especially in the south: Gades[59] and Castulo.[60] It became widely used, and even appears on a Roman coin, a quadrans from one of the first issues of bronze coins to be minted.[61]

On the coins of Emporion, the crescent moon replaces the laurel wreath, which in some issues appears above the bull on semises.

SYMBOLS

On the bronze coins of Emporion symbols are used to differentiate between the issues. The forms they take, however, are determined by the models from which they were copied, rather than by the need to distinguish between and keep an account of the issues.

The symbols used on these coins are, in order of appearance: the dolphin, cornucopia, bull, jug, palm, victory and prow. None of these are innovations; they were all used previously in other mints, particularly for Roman denarii.

THE DOLPHIN. This symbol was widely used throughout the Greek Mediterranean, and in Emporion itself three dolphins surround the head of Arethusa on the drachmas, and also in some issues the dolphin appears below the Pegasus. In the Iberian coinage of Catalonia it is used by some mints to indicate the value of the sextans[62] and at Saguntum it is to be found on the reverse of the many fractional coins.[63]

THE CORNUCOPIA. This is the sign of plenty and its horn represents material prosperity. It was widely used on ancient coins, and the closest model occurs on Roman denarii[64] and on Iberian coins from Kese in Catalonia.[65]

THE BULL. This sign appears on the reverse of coins of Emporion to indicate the value of the semis; its use as a symbol in front of the Pegasus has a precedent in Roman denarii[66] and bronze coins.[67] It also appears on more recent Iberian coins from Ore.[68]

THE JUG. This term is preferred to "amphora", since the vessel has only one handle. Amongst Roman silver coins it appears on an issue of didrachms[69] and on the denarii of SEX.POM.FOSTULUS in 137 B.C.[70] It is found with two handles, and would therefore be more correctly termed "amphora", on Iberian coins from Kese[71] and Eusti.[72]

THE PALM. The palm was very widely used in Hispania with a symbolic meaning, and it appears, held by a rider, on the reverses of many of the Iberian coins. Its origin lies in the myth of the Dioscuri. It appears on Roman denarii of CN.BLASTO[73] and C.SULP.[74] In Hispania it appears on coins from the mints of Lauro,[75] Iltirkesken,[76] Kese,[77] Ausesken[78] and Ieso.[79]

VICTORY - PROW. The Greek goddess Nike appears very widely on coins from the Greek period on. This motif was used for a Roman coin and its name, the victoriatus, also appears on ancient denarii[80] and bronze coins.[81]

At Emporion the figure of Nike is to be found on the first drachmas, placed above the standing horse like a crown, and later it was used as a symbol on some of the drachmas of the later issues.[82]

On the bronze coins of Emporion the Nike is sometimes alone and sometimes beside a ship's prow, which can only indicate naval power. The prow appears alone on some other issues.

EPIGRAPHY

Epigraphy, used to determine the evolution of the characters of the Iberian alphabet, is one of the main criterion for classifying Iberian coins.

In our material, the Iberian word UNTIKESKEN has three variants of the letters KE;

Old KE, with a dash coming from the top, inscriptions 1 and 2.
New KE, with no dash, inscriptions 3 and 4.
Archaic KE, with a dash coming from the bottom, inscription 5.

The latter form appears on the latest Iberian issues in a deliberate return to archaic forms.

The letter TI, although less conclusive than the previous one, also occurs in three variants:

Archaic TI, with the three tips paralleled, inscriptions 1 and 5.
Old TI, with the three tips open, inscriptions 2 and 3.
New TI, with the three tips coming from the same point, inscription 4.

These variants will be used as criteria for classifying the different issues.

VALUE MARKS

In the issues whose obverses have the word UNTIKESKEN in front of the head of Pallas, the reverses have inscriptions for which various interpretations have been suggested, the most usual being that they are magistrate's names. We believe them to be value marks.[84]

Our argument is twofold; we have used a widely based metrological study to obtain the values of the coins, which are confirmed by our interpretation of the inscriptions. In the present chapter only the interpretation of the inscriptions will be given, and this will be confirmed later by the metrology.

᛭ X I ᛙ and its abbreviation ᛭ I . Inscriptions 6 and 7

We interpret this inscription[85] according to the Greek number system, where E is the fifth letter in the alphabet and represents five, while I is the tenth letter and stands for ten. Consequently we interpret the sign as meaning 15, which is confirmed in issue no. 45, where the Latin XV, which indisputably represents this value, is found beside this mark.[86]

The long form of this inscription has the E and I connected by a link which we read as Iberian TA; for its interpretation we have had recourse to its similarity to Basque, in which language this conjunction means "and".

As for the final Iberian N, we suggest that it may be the initial letter of Nummus, which brings us to the interpretation 5 and 10 Nummus, which as we shall see in the chapter on metrology means that 15 of these coins equal a Roman pound.

The only objection so far proposed to this hypothesis was made by Untermann,[88] who cites a coin, no. 21 in our catalogue, which appears from the typology to be a semis, but which has this inscription. This is a single piece from the Gabinete Numismático de Cataluña, which, according to its typology, should have the inscription ETAR. Upon examining the coin, we think that the reading is uncertain, and in the unlikely event of it being a correct reading it could be a faulty coin of which only one minting was made before it was withdrawn.

᛭ X ᛤ Inscription 8

The interpretation of this inscription proved more difficult, and we followed an inverse method. Metrological studies show that 25 coins of this issue equal a Roman pound, and this should be reflected in the system of value marks, as we found to be true in the previous case.

For the inscription to have the value 25, the R must represent 20, given that the E is 5, and TA the conjunction.

In the Greek number system, R does not normally have this value, but Fevrier[89] gives three different Greek number systems, and in one of them, the least used, the R represents 20.

Untermann has raised an objection[90] to this interpretation. He believes that certain coins of this issue may be read differently, since the second sign

TA, which is a cross with horizontal arms, has on one coin a vertical line which changes it to BO. There are five coins listed in our catalogue from issue no. 20, all with the same die for the reverse and possibly also for the obverse, which suggests that only one die was made with this peculiarity, which may have been an error or a defect in the die.

ⴲ Ө ◁ Ө ◁ and its abbreviation ⴲ. Inscriptions 10 and 11

The complete word, which we read as ETERTER, appears on coins of issues nos. 16 and 22, and represents the value of a half in both series, which are parallel but belong to different metrological systems, and are characterized by having the ethnic on the obverse. The abbreviation E appears on most of the semises with the reverse of the bull.

The only possible way to interpret this was to use the parallels with Basque,[91] and in fact we find that in Basque ERDI means half, so that if we transpose the R the two words seem to be from a common root; that is both ERDI and ERTERTER may derive from a common source.

ⴲ — Inscription 12

The Iberian letter E, followed by a dash, always occurs on coins of the value of a quarter or quadrans. It would thus appear that E, which is the abbreviation for a half, means half of a half, or a quarter, when it is followed by a dash.

We have found no precedent in Greek or Latin epigraphy to support this view, but in this case the metrology is evidence enough.

M ⴲ Ϙ ʃ ◁ Inscription 13. ⟩ ⴲ M ⊘ Inscription 14, and its abbreviation M, inscription 15

These two inscriptions, which we read as SERGIR and SESTE[92] occur on the reverse of coins with the ethnic on the obverse, issues nos. 18 and 24. Their weight, as we shall see in the chapter on Metrology, is a sixth of the value of one unit, and this is confirmed by the presence of two pellets in issue no. 18, this being the Roman mark for the sextans.

Both words have the same root, which is also the root of the Latin word SEXTANTE; and Basque too has similar words for "sixth"; SEIEN and SEIGARREN. All these words appear to derive from a common source and to have the same basic meaning, although with differences of detail, as is indicated by the different endings.

GRAFFITO

The graffito, Inscription 23, which is to be found on the coin in the Villoldo Collection from issue no. 46, is read by us as[93] AR.TAV/[A]BAL[TA].

Guadan, with some reservations, interprets this as "AHI ESTA" (here it is), and Villoldo suggests that as the Basque word for wine is artau, it might mean the quantity of wine the coin would buy. Against this hypothesis is a fact that the word is divided by a full stop.

Untermann[94] suggests the reading: AR.TAN/ABALTA.

The graffito is very carefully written, as if a sculptor were working in marble, and the triangular full stop which separates the characters on the first line is of the Roman period.

MAGISTRATES

In Iberian Script

In some of the issues included in our series 7, we find names in Iberian script which are neither ethnics, nor place-names, nor value marks, and which must, without any doubt, be the names of the magistrates in charge of finance who were responsible for the issue.

Although we do not know why, we know that during part of the second century B.C., all the most important mints in Hispania produced coins inscribed with names. There must have been a fairly short period when the magistrates were authorised by the Roman authorities to have their own names inscribed on coins. This happened at Arse-Saguntum, Valentia and Obulco as well as at Emporion.

The names which appear on the coins of Emporion are:[95]

    ISKERBELES,   inscription 16
    ILTIRARKER,   inscription 17
    ATABELS,   inscription 18
    TIBERI,   inscription 19
    LVKI,   inscription 20

ISKERBELES and ATABELS both have the suffix BELES, which is very common in Iberian names. Indibal, which is Andobeles in Polybius's version[96] has this suffix, which is also found on the bronze plate of Ascoli:[97] Bennabels, Sanibelser, Beles, Umarbeles and Estobeles: Iscorbeles is a magistrate for Saguntum.[98] We also know Aenibali, Corbeli, Neintibeles and Ildubelar.[99]

The name ISKER is attested by Untermann[100] and Atabels had already been interpreted by Gomez Moreno and Tovar y Palomar.[101]

As for ILTIRARKER, the ending -ER appears in names on the bronze plate of Ascoli,[102] and ILTIR is also found in names.[103]

TIBERI is quite certainly a Latin name written in Iberian script.

LVKI

Untermann[104] gives this reading although the first letter is not at all clear. The strokes are very short for an L and the letter is almost like an Iberian V without the vertical stroke. The fact that this word is next to the value mark 15 makes it unlikely that it is itself a value mark, although it does not necessarily follow that it is a magistrate's name. However, if the reading LVKI is correct, it does seem likely to be a magistrate's name, for it would be a Latin name written in Iberian script.

The occurrence of this inscription on issue 26, with the symbol of a bull in front of Pegasus and the prow behind the head of Pallas, which is metrologically half issue 25, which also has the symbol of the bull, suggests that the word may have a meaning which we have been unable to interpret. Provisionally we may take it to be a magistrate's name.

In Latin Script

There are many magistrates' names on the coins of Emporion with Latin inscriptions. On the issue which we believe to be the earliest, the office of the magistrate appears instead of his name.

QVAIS. This inscription, which first appears as a countermark on issue 71, and is afterwards included in the die for issue 72, was previously read by us as QVAIC,[105] and interpreted as QVINQVENAL, although we said that this interpretation was very difficult to explain.

Since then we have studied more coins and found some with the word QVAIS absolutely clear, and as the last letter is an S, there is no doubt that the correct interpretation is QVAISTOR = QVESTOR, as suggested by Hubner some years ago.[106] AI often becomes AE in Latin and also in many Iberian words when these are Latinized: Baitolo=Baetulo; Aidil=Aedil; etc.

Our reading of the last letter as C, which is what it looks like on some of the coins, can be explained if C is considered to be a variant of the Greek sigma, as found in the issues of the LOGGOSTALETON, where the Greek sigma appears on the oldest coins and C on the later ones.[107]

Interpretation of Q. In the issues which follow those inscribed with QVAIS the abbreviated names of the magistrates are followed by the letter Q. It seems logical that, if we accept the interpretation Quaestor for the previous issue, Q also stands for this office.

The eminent epigrapher Professor Pflaum has stated categorically that in epigraphy Q can only stand for QVAESTOR.

When two names of magistrates appear on our coins, it would seem there were two QVAESTORES in Emporion, but we will leave this problem to the experts.

Magistrates' Names. After studying the inscriptions of magistrates' names on numerous coins, and carefully noting the punctuation which separates the letters or groups of letters, we find that there are some coins with four names and some with six, and only two with five.

We believe that they designate two magistrates, who sometimes have two names each and sometimes three.

In the earliest issues the magistrates each have two names. There is only one case of the same magistrates being designated by two and by three names in the same issue, the third name being the one omitted when there are only two, and not the second as would be normal Roman practice.

The fact that the magistrates are designated by two names, in Greek fashion, surely reflects the Greek origins of the city and of the way its inhabitants were named, which must have lasted through the city's progressive Romanization.

These methods of naming are also seen on two stone tablets found in Emporion, one bearing the name Democritos Sostraton, or Democritos son of Sostraton,[108] and the other, Tespi Aristoleon Messaleita, or Tespi son of Aristoleon of Massalia.[109]

With the increasing Romanization that followed Caesar's installation of the colonists, the magistrates came to be designated in the Roman way, by praenomen, nomen, and cognomen.

Pairs of Magistrates Designated by Two Names

    C.I. - L.C.   issues 73-74
    P.L. - L.L.   issues 75-76
    L.C. - C.R.   issue 80
    M.O. - L.A.   issue 90

Pairs of Magistrates Designated by Three Names

P.I.P.	- C.S.M.	issue 83-84
C.P.C.	- M.S.R.	issue 88
M.O.H.	- L.A.F.	issue 91-92
P.C.PV	- Q.C.C.	issue 93
C.S.B.	- L.C.M.	issue 94
CN.C.P.	- C.M.A.	issue 95-96
CN.C.GR.	- L.C.F(A).	issue 97-98
C.CA.T.	- C.O.CA(R).	issue 99-100
C.T.C.	- Q.C.CA.	issue 101
C.O.C.	- C.M.A.	issue 102-103
M.A.B.	- M.F.M.	issue 104-105-106

Pairs of Magistrates in which one is Designated by Three Names and the other by Two

    C.I.NICOM.- P.FL.   issue 85-86
    L.M.RUF. - P.C.   issue 89

Remarks: We note that L.C. and C.M.A. were both magistrates twice.

Some apparently different magistrates may be the same, being designated at one time by two names and at another by the same two names plus a third.

Such is certainly the case with M.O. - L.A. and M.O.H. - L.A.F. and may also be true of C.I. and C.I. NICOM, L.C. and L.C.F. or L.C.M., C.O.C. and C.O.CAR.

For the two exceptional cases, the following interpretations are suggested:

C.I. NICOM - P.FL., who appear on issue 85 and issue 86, where P.FL is repeated on the reverse. In epigraphy FL is short for Flamen, and P may stand for Primus, which would give Flamen Primus.

L.M.RVF., followed by P.C., has already been interpreted by Heiss,[110] who explains that when the Emperor accepted a municiple office, there was only one magistrate and his office was expressed by some formula, such as in this case P.C., which could stand for PRAEFECTVS CAESARIS or PROCVRATOR CAESARIS.[111]

On one lead plate from the Ballesta necropolis, the name of Rufus, legatus Augusti appears amongst those of cursed persons. He could well be the Rufus whose name appears on the coins.

L.M.RVF. could stand for Lucius Marcus Rufus[113] or L. Mescinius Rufus, "triumvir of the mint" in Rome in the year 16 B.C.[114]

COUNTERMARKS

Almost all the coins of Emporion which are countermarked have in fact two countermarks, one with a dolphin in a circle, which is always placed above Pallas's helmet, and another rectangular one with the letters D.D., placed in front of her face.

Exceptionally, we find coins with these countermarks randomly placed and very exceptionally, coins with different countermarks.

It must be emphasised that of the countermarked coins found on the site of Emporion, all, without exception, are marked with the dolphin and D.D. The few coins with different countermarks must have had these applied in other places.

We know of only one example of a coin which has magistrates' names and is countermarked with a dolphin and D.D. Only two examples are known to us of coins of issues 81 and 82, without magistrates' names, countermarked with the dolphin and the letters D.D. All the other countermarked coins, which make up our issues 110 and 111, are coins without the names of magistrates from issues 107 and 109.

The distinction is quite clear; only certain coins were countermarked, to be precise, those from later issues without magistrates' names. As previously stated, 55 coins of the old issue without magistrates' names are known, and only 2 are countermarked which must be in error.

The two stamps of the dolphin and the letters D.D. were applied with the greatest care; the dolphin, the emblem of the city, over the helmet, and D.D., an abbreviation of <u>Decreto Decurionum,</u> a sign of authority, in front of the figure.

The fact that only coins without magistrates' names were countermarked suggests that these coins needed something to make them fully legal, and that stamping them with D.D. gave them a mark of authority which ensured their value and legality.

The coins with countermarks in unusual places, or with one of the stamps missing or repeated, are included in series 26 of issue 112.

The other countermarks known to us on coins of Emporion are described in the catalogue in series 27, issues no. 113-121.

METROLOGY

We have revised our previous work on the metrology of the bronze coins of Emporion.[116] As our present material is almost twice as large, we have been able to be more precise than was then possible.

For the metrological study of the series from Emporion we have used Henry's method[117] to check their homogeneity, and plotted the respective curves.

In every case the homogeneity of the series is evident, with the single exception of some semises, which are unusual in having an average weight less than that expected in relation to the corresponding asses. These are the semises of series 6, 7, 8 and 9.

The subsequent series either have no semises or so few that it is impossible to draw any conclusions about them.

The most modern semises with Iberian inscriptions, which we have placed in series 14 and which belong to issues no. 61, 62 and 63, do have a correct average weight, but Henry's method demonstrates that they are not sufficiently homogeneous wholes.

Apart from these few exceptions, all the other series are metrologically correct, and we give below their average weights, with, in brackets, the number of coins of known weight from which this average was obtained.

A - SYSTEM OF 15 COINS TO THE ROMAN POUND

Series 1-9, except for 4, which has 25 coins to the Roman pound.

Series 1, 2, 3 and 5.   Fractions with correct weights in relation to the unit.

AS, nos. 1, 5, 11, 12, 13, 15 and 25: average weight 21.97 g (129)

SEMIS, nos. 2, 3, 6, 9 and 16: average weight 10.68 g (95)

QUADRANS, no. 7, 10, 14 and 17: average weight 5.08 g (78)

SEXTANS, nos. 4 and 8: average weight 3.81 g (24)

Total average weight 21.46 (325) x 15 = 321.98 g.

Series 6.   Fractions with a lower than expected weight in relation to the unit.

AS, nos. 27, 28, 29, 30 and 31: average weight 18.81 g (44)

SEMIS, no. 32: average weight 6.61 g (9)

Series 7. Fractions with a lower than expected weight in relation to the unit.

AS, no. 33: average weight 20.60 g (3)

SEMIS, nos. 34, 36 and 37: average weight 7.38 g (18)

QUADRANS, no. 35: average weight 3.79 g (11)

Series 8. Fractions with a lower than expected weight in relation to the unit.

AS, no. 39: average weight 21.17 g (65)

SEMIS, no. 40: average weight 8.30 g (11)

QUADRANS, no. 41: average weight 2.57 g (3)

Series 9. Fractions with a lower than expected weight in relation to the unit.

AS, nos. 42 and 45: average weight 21.24 g (93)

SEMIS, no. 43: average weight 8.63 g (13)

QUADRANS, no. 44: average weight 3.21 g (2)

Total average weight series 1 to 9, except 4 = 21.17 (333) x 15 = 317.55 g. Discrepancy with the pound = 2.8%.

It is clear that all early asses of Emporion were minted according to a metrological system that diverges from the contemporary Roman one, which was the uncial system of 27.2 g.

Series 1, which has no value marks, has an average weight of 24.54 g for its 18 coins, which is more than our weight but less than the uncial. In the next issue of asses, 5, the average weight of 22.44 g is very close to the one we give.

Metrologically, 15 of these coins weigh exactly one Roman pound,[118] and this number, which shows the size of the coin, is in most issues stamped on the obverse, in front of Pallas's face. It is possible that coins of the early issues which do not have any value marks were already produced according to this system, and that the mark was introduced subsequently to register something that was already being done.

Traditionally this mark, made up of two signs, has been read as the Iberian characters EBA, whereas it is in fact a value mark[119] which, according to the Greek number system, denotes 15, as is proved by issue no. 45, where the Latin numerals XV also appear.[120]

In series 3, we have interpreted the value mark which appears on the exergue on the reverse, and which was previously read as Iberian EDABAN, as 15 nummus, that is 15 of these coins to the Roman pound.[121] This hypothesis was explained in a previous chapter.

As stated, the average weight of 332 of these asses is 21.17 g, which, multiplied by 15, gives 317.55 g, differing from the Roman pound of 326.4 g by only 2.8%, which may well be wastage. The coincidence is perfect and complete.

For the semises, which have the value of half a unit, and the bull stamp on the reverse, the value mark is normally an Iberian E, but in series 3, issue 16 has on its reverse the Iberian inscription ETERTER, which we interpret, as explained in a previous chapter, as a half, by analogy with Basque.

From the table of weights it is clear that the coins with this mark or its abbreviation E from issues 3, 6, 9 and 16, with an average weight of 10.65 g, are exactly half the as of 21.17 g.

For the quadrans or quarter, with a lion on the reverse, the value mark is an Iberian E followed by a dash, which must mean a quarter, as the metrological evidence shows, for in issues nos. 7, 10, 14 and 17 this coin has an average weight of 5.08 g, which is exactly a quarter of 21.17 g.

For the sextans the mark is an Iberian S on issues nos. 4 and 8, this being the first letter of the word SERGIR which appears on coins of issue 18, with a horse's head on the reverse. The average weight of these coins is 3.81 g, exactly one sixth of the weight of the as.

B - THE SYSTEM WITH 25 COINS TO THE ROMAN POUND

Running parallel to series 3 with the ethnic on the obverse is another series with this characteristic, series 4, with inscriptions on the reverse which we interpret as value marks.

The same inscriptions appear in both series, and although the coins are of different weights they have the same value in relation to their respective units.

Series 3 and 4 are clearly differentiated from each other by their style, but each is homogeneous as regards the coins of different values which form the series.

Series 4, with 25 coins to the Roman pound.

UNIT, nos. 19, 20 and 21: average weight 12.07 g (26)

HALF, nos. 19, 20 and 21: average weight 12.07 g (26)

QUARTER, no. 23: average weight 3.29 g (36)

SIXTH, no. 24: average weight 2.08 g (3)

Total average weight 12.86 (108) x 25 = 321.50. Discrepancy with the pound = 1.5%.

The interpretation of the inscription as a value mark, ETAR standing for 25, which we have already suggested, is metrologically confirmed here.

There are similar confirmations that the inscription ETERTER in issue 22 stands for a half, that the inscription E - in issue 23 means a quarter, and that the inscription SESTE in issue 24 designates a sixth.

C - REDUCED UNCIAL SYSTEM

The series from Emporion 10, 11 and 12 show the following pattern of weights:

Series 10 and 11

AS, nos. 46 to 49, 51 and 52: average weight 16.05 g (45)

SEMIS, no. 50: average weight 8.22 g (1)

Series 12

AS, nos. 53 to 55, 57 and 58: average weight 15.01 g (75)

SEMIS, no. 56: average weight 10.14 g (3)

The total average weight is 15.40 g (120), which must correspond to one of the reductions in weight of the Roman as, possibly a reduction arising from the re-valuation of the denarius at 16 asses.

Previously, the denarius equalled 10 asses of 27.2 g, or 272 g.

The new denarius was to weigh 272 divided by 16 = 16 g, which is approximately two thirds of the Roman uncia.[122]

The average weights of these series are slightly below those expected, and may correspond to one of the subsequent reductions.

We would suggest that if the librum was divided into 15 in previous issues, here it could have been divided into 20, and then 326.4 divided by 20 = 16.32 g.

The four semises which are all we have from these series are not enough to prove anything.

D - REDUCED SEMIUNCIAL SYSTEM

We give below the table of weights for subsequent issues, up to the end of those with Iberian inscriptions:

Series 13

AS, nos. 59 and 60: average weight 11.71 g (27)

Series 14

SEMIS, nos. 61, 62 and 63: average weight 6.08 g (34)

Series 15

AS, no. 64: average weight 9.72 g (2)

Series 16

AS, no. 65 to 68: average weight 11.11 g (112)

Total average weight is 11.39 (175), which does not exactly fit the Roman semiuncial system,[123] and is in fact lighter. We may assume that even if this system follows the Roman one, the weights are lighter as usually happened when the system was introduced into Hispania.

E - AUGUSTAN SYSTEM

All the coins from Emporion with Latin inscriptions conform exactly to the same metrological system, as is shown by the metrological data which follow:

Series 17, AS, no. 69: average weight 10.92 g (47)
Series 18, AS, nos. 70 to 72: average weight 10.98 g (36)
Series 19, AS, nos. 73 to 76 and 80: average weight 10.18 g (57)
Series 20, AS, nos. 81 and 82: average weight 9.38 g (48)
Series 21, AS, no. 83 to 86 and 88: average weight 9.94 g (46)
Series 22, AS, no. 89: average weight 10.49 (30)
Series 23, AS, nos. 90 to 93: average weight 10.65 g (29)
Series 24, AS, nos. 94 to 106: average weight 10.27 g (89)
Series 25, AS, nos. 107 and 109: average weight 10.41 g (67)
Series 26, AS, nos. 110 to 112: average weight 10.22 g (146)
Series 27, AS, nos. 113 to 121: average weight 9.76 g (5)

Average total weight of the asses 10.28 g (599)

Fraction nos. 77 to 79: average weight 1.66 g (54)

Fraction no. 87: average weight 1.83 g (15)

The average weight of these fractions is 1.697 (69), which multiplied by 6 equals 10.18, showing them to be sextantes.

Fraction no. 108: average weight 2.53 (19)

Fraction no. 122: average weight 2.58 (20)

The average weight of these fractions is 2.555 g (39), which multiplied by 4 equals 10.22 g showing them to be quadrantes.

From this table of weights we can deduce that the as conforms to the Augustan system introduced into Rome in about 20 B.C., which has 30 asses to the Roman pound.

The fractions ceased to be sextantes and became quadrantes in conformity with the Augustan system whose only fraction is the quadrans.

FINDS OF COINS

Very little data is furnished by finds of coins from Emporion, and what data there it is somewhat negative, for there are no coins of this type in the hoards of Balsareny[124] or Cànoves,[125] which indicates that the circulation of coins from Emporion in Vallès at the end of the second century B.C. was nil or very small. The northwards spread of the coins of Emporion was always more rapid; in Catalonia they are found only on the coast.[126]

The few coins found in contexts which may give some indication as to their chronology are listed below:

NUMANTIA.[127] In camp 3 of Renieblas, in use in the period 153-137 B.C., two bronze coins of Emporion were found with Roman coins of the period 208-150. They are:

Haeberlin 129, our issue no. 1, Mainz - Hill II-I
Haeberlin 128, our issue no. 16

Two coins of our issues nos. 2 and 25, which came originally from the Numantian camps, were in the old Moneteverde collection, and are now in the Balsach.

EMPORION. In the Martí necropolis,[128] together with three Roman asses, one anonymous, one of M. TITINI and one of Q. MARC. LIBO, of the period 208-150 B.C., were found 4 asses with Iberian inscriptions minted in Emporion. These are nos. 221, 204, 1109 and 293 of the Museo Arqueológico de Barcelona, and belong to our issues nos. 5, 12, 12, and 25 respectively.

EMPORION 1972.[129] This small hoard awaits further study and publication. Together with an anonymous Roman as of 28.62 g, and a semis of the type Crawford no. 196/2, of the period 169-158 B.C., 38 bronze coins of Emporion were found:

Issue no. 39, MAB 1530, one piece
Issue no. 42, MAB 1508 to 1528, twenty one pieces
Issue no. 43, MAB 1529, one piece

These are from two issues which we had already placed in relation to each other, each of them having a semis. This find confirms our relative placing, the coins from issue no. 42-43 being better preserved.

AZAILA.[130] In the Iberian oppidum of Cabezo de Alcalé de Azaila, two hoards of coins were found, comprising 713 coins in all. Amongst these were two from Emporion with Iberian inscriptions, nos. 689 and 690 of the MAN.[131] Because of their poor state of preservation they were not very accurately described; they belong respectively to our issues 42 and 25.

These treasures were hidden during the Sertorian Wars, which provides us with a terminus ante quem. The state of wear of the coins is similar to that of the asses of the Roman Uncial system found in the same hoard.

To our knowledge no coins of Emporion with Latin inscriptions have been found in any hoards; the only one we can cite was found in the Ballesta necropolis in Emporion,[132] no. 1085 of the MAB, our issue no. 81, which was found with a bronze coin of Octavian inscribed CAESAR DIVI.F, the reverse showing the head of Caesar crowned with a laurel wreath and the words DIVVS IULIVS, dating from 40-27 B.C.[133]

CLASSIFICATION CRITERIA

SERIES WITH IBERIAN INSCRIPTIONS

For these series, we start by using epigraphical and metrological criteria.

Judging by epigraphy,[134] the earliest are series 1 to 5, with <u>old KE</u>. These are followed by series 6 to 14, with <u>later KE</u>. In the latest of the Iberian issues, series 15 to 16, the epigraphy shows a deliberate archaizing tendency, and we find the three types of KE appearing in one issue, which also shows other deliberate archaisms: the Pegasus with a normal head, the laurel wreath placed above the horse's hind quarters, and the use of a value mark.

Turning now to metrology, we find that the early issues used the system of 15 coins to the Roman pound, which is found in series 1 to 9. A reduction in weight began in series 10 to 12, when a system of 20 coins to the pound was introduced, and for series 13 to 18 a system slightly heavier than the Roman semiuncial was adopted. These criteria enable us to draw up an initial classification:

Epigraphy	Metrology	Series
old KE	15 coins to the pound	1, 2, 3 and 5
later KE		6, 7, 8 and 9
	20 coins to the pound	10, 11 and 12
	reduced semiuncial	13, 14 and 15
later, old and archaic KE		16

Out of the first five series, for reasons of style we place the series where Pallas's helmet is round and made in one piece before the one where her helmet is made up of two sections. This placing matches the criterion that the issues without symbols and without value marks are the first ones.

Round helmet	with neither value mark or symbol	issues 1 to 4
	with laurel wreath	issues 5 to 8
	with symbols	issues 9 to 10
Helmet in sections	with no value mark	issues 11 to 12
	with value mark	issues 13 to 14

We place next the two parallel series 3 and 4, which, although their metrological systems are different, have the ethnic on the obverse and the value mark on the reverse; they are stylistically inferior to the preceding series and they have the archaic form of the letter TI.

Next we place series 5 with the symbol of the bull in front of Pegasus.

When classifying series 6 to 9 with later KE we place first those series which are stylistically linked to the preceding series. Amongst these we put first issue 27, which has no value mark and after these the group which has a caduceus in the exergue, that is, issues 28 to 30.

Next comes a typological change, the position of the laurel wreath above the Pegasus being moved from above the hind quarters to between the wings and the head. This occurs in issues 31 and 32.

We place next the issues with magistrates' names, nos. 33 to 38.

Next come the issues with the laurel wreath in front of the wings, and the value mark, nos. 39 to 41; and those which add the jug symbol, nos. 42 to 45.

When classifying series 10 to 12, with a metrological system of 20 asses to the pound, we place first no. 10 which has the laurel wreath in front of the wings, and later those which have the laurel wreath above the hind quarters, which is a return to a previous position. These later series are no. 11, with no symbol, and no. 12 with Nike and the prow.

When classifying series 13 to 16, with a reduced semiuncial metrological system, we place first no. 13 where the Pegasus has a Kabeirus head and afterwards the others where the Pegasus has a normal head.

SERIES WITH LATIN INSCRIPTIONS

We have divided these series into several groups, and have used several different criteria to determine their sequence.

A. Inscription MUNICI EMPORIA, with Diana on the obverse.
B. Series of the same type and Iberian style with or without QVAIS, countermarked or included on the die.
C. Pairs of magistrates with two names each.
D. Pairs of magistrates with three names each.
E. Those without names of magistrates.

Group A is totally unrelated to any others, and therefore very difficult to place. These coins may have been minted at the time the Municipium was founded, and be unrelated to any preceding or subsequent issues. They make up our series 17, which we have placed at the head of the Latin series.

Group B is the one whose style is Iberian, and it therefore seems linked to the last issues with Iberian inscriptions, which is why, in a previous study, we placed it immediately after these. Now, however, we consider it more likely to have followed the issues with Munici and preceded those with magistrates' names, and it makes up our series 18.

Group C with magistrates with two names each is still largely Iberian in style like the preceding series. Its epigraphy shows the open Iberian P in the names C.I.L.C. and P.L.L.L., while in L.C.C.R. the style has evolved towards that of the subsequent issues, showing the Pegasus with wings curled forward.

These three issues make up our series 19 and in this we include the fractional currency, which is stylistically similar. The fractions do not have names of magistrates and have only the first letters of the legend: EMP, EM or IM.

Of the issues without magistrates' names, one is stylistically linked to the previous issue with the names L.C.C.R., and to the subsequent issue with the names P.I.P.C.S.M., with which it has some reverses in common.

It is clear that this issue without magistrates' names is earlier than the others which have no names and which we have placed at the end of the Latin series, both because of its completely different style and because of the almost complete absence of countermarks, present in only one coin of this issue; whereas the majority of coins from the issues at the end of the series are countermarked.

Group D, of magistrates with three names each, is headed by the issue with the names P.I.P.C.S.M., which is linked by a common reverse to the preceding issue 20.

We place next the issue of C.I.NICOM.P.FL., which is identical in style, and then the issue of C.P.C.M.S.R.

Also in this group of issues we place some fractional currency of the same style, with the Pegasus wings curved strongly forward, and without names of magistrates.

Series 22, which comes next and consists of one issue only, is stylistically very close to the preceding ones, but with a smaller head, and is unusual in having only one magistrates' name: L.M.RVF.

Series 23 shows a further evolution of the style of series 22, and one issue is unusual in that the magistrates sometimes have two names and sometimes three: M.O.L.A. and M.O.H.L.A.F.

We close this series with the issue of P.C.PV.Q.C.C.

Series 24 is made up of the remaining seven pairs of magistrates with three names each, in which a new style is seen developing into several characteristic types. This style affects not only the head of Minerva, but also the Pegasus.

The sequence of these issues is determined purely on stylistic grounds, which is possibly too subjective a criterion, although it is at least certain that the issues we have placed last are closest to the ones without magistrates' names which close our series of coins of Emporion. A discussion of these follows.

THE LAST ISSUES WITHOUT MAGISTRATES NAMES

We believe that issues nos. 107 and 109 were the last to be minted in Emporion, and base this belief not only on stylistic criteria, which are always subjective, but on the halving and countermarking of the coins of Emporion. These criteria also enable us to place the series in their correct order; 107 with a small head precedes 109 with a larger head and this order is confirmed by the halving and countermarking of coins.

The halving of coins[135] provides data which has enabled us to draw up the following table:

Issue	Coins			Percentage of the halved coins in proportion to the total
	Halved	Whole	Total	
107	5	43	48	10
109	9	31	40	22
110	3	54	57	5
111	30	120	150	20
107 - 110	8	97	105	7
109 - 111	39	151	190	20

In issue 107, 10% of coins were halved before the countermark was applied, and only 5% after.

In issue 109, 22% of the coins were halved before being countermarked and 20% after they were countermarked. This shows that coins were already being halved when issue 109 was minted and that they went on being halved after this. Besides issue 107 is earlier than issue 109, as is shown by comparing the number of coins halved and left whole in the two issues, 7% of the first and 20% of the second being halved.

The use of the countermark is shown by the following table:

	without countermarks		with countermarks			% with countermarks
	issue	no. of coins	issue	no. coins	total	
Catalogue no.	107	48	110	57	105	54
	109	40	111	150	190	78
From the excavations at Emporion	109	6	111	66	72	83

This shows that the countermark was applied after both issues were minted and that the later issue is 109, which has the most coins with countermarks.

Of the coins of issue 109 which are from the excavations at Emporion, 83% have countermarks, which would seem to suggest that all coins without magistrates' names which were in circulation in the city had to be countermarked.

The order we suggest is:
      (i)   Issue 107 ... halving of coins
      (ii)   Issue 109 ... halving of coins continues
      (iii) Countermark introduced   halving of coins continues

CHRONOLOGY

Having established a sequence, or relative chronology, on the basis of various criteria, it now remains to propose an absolute chronology. With this end in view we will first see if any chronological data can be obtained from coins found in hoards, and then compare the metrology with that of contemporary Roman coins of known date. The issues inscribed with magistrates' names will be of some assistance, as will the Munici Emporia issue; and the countermarking and halving of coins will enable us to place the end of the issues. On the basis of all this a chronology will be suggested.

FINDS OF COINS

The scanty data provided by finds enables us to make only the following deductions:

Series 1 to 3   = issues 1 to 16: before 153-137 B.C.

Series 1 to 5   = issues 5 to 25: contemporary with Roman currency of the period 208-150 B.C.

Series 8 to 9   = issues 39 to 42: after 169-158 B.C.

Series 5 to 9   = issues 25 to 43: before 72 B.C.

Series 20   = issue 81: was in circulation at the same time as a coin of 40-27 B.C.

METROLOGY

Although the asses of our series 1 to 9 had a distinctive pattern of 15 coins to the Roman pound, they are close to the Roman uncial as, with which they must be contemporary, and which was introduced at the beginning of the second century B.C. The reduction in weight of this system in series 10, 11 and 12 must be contemporary with that of the Roman uncial as when the denarius was revalued around 143 B.C.[136]

The reduction of the Roman bronze coinage to the semi-uncial system in around 91 B.C.[137] must have been simultaneous with the further reduction in weight of the coins of Emporion of series 13 and 14, where a reduced semi-uncial system was introduced.

All the Latin issues of Emporion, from series 17 to the end, follow the Augustan system and must therefore be later than 27 B.C., the year when this new system was introduced.

This gives us the following chronological data:

Series 1 to 9: system of 15 asses to the pound: beginning of the second century B.C.

Series 10 to 12: reduced uncial system: around 143 B.C.

Series 13 to 16: reduced semi-uncial system: around 91 B.C.

Series 17 to end: Augustan system: after 27 B.C.

THE MUNICI EMPORIA ISSUE

This issue, unique both in its inscription and in its representation of Diana, may correspond to a particular event, such as the founding of the municipium, and be unrelated to any other issues.

The obverse with Diana marks a radical change in the typology of Emporion, and recalls a similar change in the issues of the Colony of Lepidus,[138] which have what has been variously interpreted as a Victoria or Venus on the obverse. This seems to be a reason for considering the two issues to be contemporary, and as the Lepidus issues date from the first government of Lepidus in 48-47 B.C. or the second in 44 B.C., we may assume that the Munici Emporia issue also dates from this time, which coincides with the founding of the Roman colony by Caesar.

If the representation of Diana is a consequence of Augustus's veneration for this goddess, as was previously suggested, this would give us the dates 36 and 14 B.C.

THE ISSUES WITH MAGISTRATES NAMES

The chronology we originally suggested for the series with Latin inscriptions must be modified, as a result of our new interpretation of the final Q which follows the magistrates names on the inscriptions. Our chronology is based not only on epigraphy but also on metrology and on a study of the coins in circulation, based on the coins found in the excavations at Emporion.

The interpretation of Q as Quaestor and not as quinquennial means that it is no longer necessary to postulate a five year interval between each of the issues with magistrates names, and as we are certain of the date when these issues ceased, we no longer have to seek their beginning around 70 B.C., which posed a very difficult metrological problem. We can now suggest a later date for the start of these issues, and the metrological problem is solved.

All the issues with magistrates names, of series 17 to 27, follow the same metrological system, with the as weighing 10.28 g, the average weight of 599 coins, which is the same weight as the Augustan as introduced about 27 B.C.

Our original interpretation forced us to conclude that this system was established in Emporion about 60/70 B.C., but we could not explain this. The new interpretation of Q, which allows us to propose a later date for the issues with magistrates' names, gives us a solution to the metrological problem.

When studying the circulation of coins in Emporion[139] on the basis of the coins from the excavations, we used a system of "coins per year", which should logically give us a regular number for the different periods.

We obtained a figure of 3.25 coins per year, for the coins belonging to Hispanic issues of the period "second century B.C. to the reign of Claudius", up to and including 54 A.D. If we take the number of coins per year for shorter periods, we find that it is 3.15 until 27 B.C., which includes the Latin issues of Emporion up to no. 9 of our previous classification.[140] For the period of Augustus we obtain a very low figure, 1.12 coins per year. For Tiberius it rises to 6.26, drops to 2.75 for Caligula (where the low figure can be explained by the damnatio memoriae), and rises again to 6.30 for Claudius.

The very low figure for the period of Augustus seems to suggest that the Latin issues of Emporion which we originally placed before Augustus may in fact belong to the reign of this Emperor, which would raise the figure of coins per year for this period, bringing it up to 2.82, while the period from the beginning of the second century to 27 B.C. would be reduced to 2.74 coins per year. This would make the figures more logical.

On combining these results with our new interpretation of QVAIS, the metrological study of the coins inscribed with magistrates names, and the circulation of coins in Emporion, we find it necessary to bring forward the date when these issues were introduced. In our opinion they are contemporary with Augustus and they must have begun to be produced in about 27 B.C.

COUNTERMARKING

Countermarking was introduced after the last two issues, without magistrates names, had been minted, and may have been more or less directly connected with the ending of local issues in Hispania, which occurred at the beginning of the reign of Claudius or perhaps even earlier, towards the end of Caligula's reign.

CHRONOLOGICAL CONCLUSIONS

On the basis of the preceding observations, we have arrived at the following conclusions, which are set out below:

After 195 B.C.	Series 1 to 7
About 169/158 B.C.	Series 8 and 9
After 143 B.C.	Series 10 to 12
After 91 B.C.	Series 13 to 16
Between 44 and 27 B.C.	Series 17
After 27 B.C.	Series 18 to 24
About 30 A.D.	Issue 107
From 30 to 35 A.D.	Issue 109
After 30 A.D.	Halving of coins

In the period of Caligula (37-41) and Claudius (41-54) - countermarking - Series 26 and 27.

CATALOGUE

To reduce the length of the catalogue, the following shortened descriptions will be used:

Pallas	=	Head of Pallas in Corinthian helmet with crest, to right.
Pegasus-Kabeirus	=	Pegasus right, with his head in the form of a small crouching figure with hands holding his feet and wearing a cap.
Pegasus	=	Pegasus right, with normal head.
Bull	=	Bull butting right.
Lion	=	Standing lion right.
Horse galloping	=	Horse galloping right.
Horse's head	=	Horse's head right.
Sea-Horse	=	Sea-Horse right.
Cock	=	Cock standing right with flower in his beak.
Wild boar	=	Wild boar right.
Wreath above croups	=	Wreath above croups, behind the wings.
Wreath before	=	Wreath between the head and wings.
Mod.	=	Module in millimetres.

The inscription, if not specified, is placed in front of Pallas's head on the obverse and beneath the Pegasus on the reverse. We note the inscription by means of an "I" and a number, referring to those in the following table of Iberian inscriptions. The Latin inscriptions will be specified in each particular case.

After each coin's description we give the module and the following bibliography:

V = A. Vives Escudero, La Moneda Hispanica, Madrid 1926.

H = G. F. Hill, Notes on the ancient coinage of Hispania Citerior, New York 1931.

V.64 = L. Villaronga, Los magistrados en las amonedaciones latinas de Emporiae, en Estudios de Numismática Romana, Barcelona 1964, 81-96.

V.72 = L. Villaronga, Sistematización del bronce ibérico emporitano, Acta Numismática II, 1972, 49-86.

GUADAN = A. M. Guadan, Tipologia de las contramarcas en la amonedación ibero-romana, Numario Hispánico IX, 1960.

The following details are given for each coin: Museum or collection, weight and die-axis.

An asterisk indicates that the coin is illustrated in the plates. In many cases there are coins illustrated with the same catalogue number. We will distinguish them by means of this number and alphabetical letters.

Abbreviations used in the Catalogue:

Botet i Sisó = J. Botet I Sisó, Les monedes catalanes, 3 vols. Barcelona 1908-11.

Delgado = A. Delgado, Nuevo método de clasificación de las medallas autonomas de España, vol. III, Seville 1876.

Pujol y Camps = C. Pujol y Camps, Empúries. Catálogo de sus monedas e imitaciones, Memorial Numismático Español III, 1873.

G N = Caceta Numismática, Asociación Numismática Española, Barcelona.

MNE = Memorial Numismático Español, I a V, Barcelona.

M A B = "Museo Arqueológico de Barcelona, coins from the excavation of Emporion.

M A T = Museo Arqueológico de Tarragona.

G N C = Gabinete Numismático de Catalunya, Barcelona.

M. Banyoles = Museo de Banyoles, Gerona.

Porqueres = oppidum Porqueres, Banyoles, Gerona.

M. Eivissa = Museo de Ibiza, Islas Baleares.

M. Mataró = Museo de Mataro, Barcelona.

M. Vic = Museu Diocessà de Vic.

M. Puig = Musée Puig de Perpignan.

MAN = J. M. Navascues, Las monedas hispánicas del Museo Arqyeológico Nacional de Madrid. I Ciclo griego e ibero-romano, Asociación Numismática Española, Barcelona, 1969.

M. del Prado = Museo del Prado, Madrid.

IVDJ = Instituto de Valencia de Don Juan, Madrid.

BM = British Museum, London.

Paris = Cabinet de Paris, Bibliothèque Nationale.

Paris, col. Luynes = Colection Luynes of Cabinet de Paris.

Condé-sur-Aisne = J. B. Giard, Le pelèrinage gallo-romain de Condé-sur-Aisne, et les monnaies, Revue Numismatique tome X, 1969, p. 103.

München SNG = <u>Sylloge Nummorum Graecorum Deutschland. Staatliche Munzsammlung Munchen,</u> 1 heft, Berlin 1968.

Corpus Christi = <u>Sylloge Nummorum Graecorum IV, the Lewis Collection in Corpus Christi College,</u> Part I, London 1972.

HSA = Hispanic Society of America, New York.

Sub. ANE = Catalogo de Subasta de la Asociación Española de Numismática, Barcelona.

Sub. Circulo = Catálogo de Subasta del Circulo Filatélico y Numismático de Barcelona.

Victor Catala = J. Maluquer de Motes, <u>La colección Arqyeológica Victor Català,</u> II, Pyrenae 3, Barcelona.

Vincke = E. Vincke, <u>Apuntes sobre la lectura de varias leyendas an monedas celtíberas,</u> Palamos 1953.

TABLE OF IBERIAN INSCRIPTIONS WITH TRANSCRIPTION

1 — UNTIKESKEN
2 — UNTIKESKEN
3 — UNTIKESKEN
4 — UNTIKESKEN
5 — UNTIKESKEN
6 — ETABAN or 15
7 — EBA or 15
8 — ETAR or 25
9 — EBOR or 25
10 — ETERTER
11 — E
12 — E-
13 — ŚEŔKIR
14 — SEŚTE
15 — Ś
16 — ISKEŔBELEŚ
17 — ILTIŔAŔKER or ILTI
18 — ATABELS
19 — TIBEŔI
20 — LVKI
21 — PHI
22 — EBA or 15 / XV
23 — AR TAU (A)BAL(TA)

We refer to private collections under the name of their owners.

We thank again all the Museum Directors and Curators and all the collectors who have furnished material for the catalogue, material which has made possible for us the work we are now offering to readers.

KEY TO CATALOGUE

IBERIAN INSCRIPTIONS

<u>Fifteen asses to one pound</u>

<u>with old KE</u>

Series 1	Round helmet	
	Without mark	1 As
		2, 3 Semis
		4 sextans
	With wreath above croup	5 As
		6 Semis
		7 Quadrans
		8 Sextans
	Smaller denominations with symbol	9 dolphin, Semis
		10 Cornucopia, Quadrans
Series 2	Lobular helmet	
	Without mark	11 As
	Wreath above croup	12 As
	With mark and wreath above croup	13 As
		14 Quadrans
Series 3	Inscription UNDIKESKEN on obverse	15 As
		16 Semis
		17 Quadrans
		18 Sextans
Series 4	Inscription UNDIKESKEN on obverse, and system of 25 units in pound	19 unit, EDAR
		20 unit, EBOR
		21 unit, EDABAN
		22 half
		23 fourth
		24 sixth
Series 5	Bull before pegasus	25 As
	and also mark	26

<u>With new KE</u>

Series 6	Same style of head	
	Without symbol	27 As
	With wreath and caduceus	27 bis As
	Caduceus winged, palm to right of the inscription	28 AS
	Caduceus to right	29 As
	Caduceus to left	30 As
	Wreath before the wings	31 As
		32 Semis
Series 7	With Iberian names of magistrates	
	ISKERBELES - ILTIRARKER	33 As
		34 Semis
		35 Quadrans
	ATABELS - TIBERI	36 Semis
		37 Quadrans
	TIBERI	38 Semis
Series 8	Wreath before wings, mark EI	39 As
		40 Semis
		41 Quadrans
Series 9	Behind jug, wreath before wings, palm to right of the inscription, mark EI	42 As
		43 Semis
		44 Quadrans
	And also mark XV	45 As

<u>Asses of two-thirds of an ounce</u>

Series 10	Wreath before, mark EI, palm to right of the inscription	46 As
Series 11	Wreath above croup	
	Palm to right of the inscription	47 As
	Pegasus with curved wings	48 As
	Helmet with straight visor	49 As
		50 Semis
	In exergue inscription	51 As
	Greek φ above pegasus	52 As
Series 12	Nike and prow	
	Round helmet	53 As
	Lateral crest	54 As
	Larger crest	55 As
		56 Semis
	Nike	57 As
	Prow	58 As

Asses of less than half an ounce

Series 13	Prow	
	Lateral crest	59 As
	Head to left	60 As
Series 14	Emissions of diverse semisses	
	Round helmet	61 Semis
	Lobular helmet	62 Semis
	With letter A	63 Semis

PEGASUS WITH NORMAL HEAD

Series 15	Nike and Prow	64 As
Series 16	Without symbol	
	With new KE	65 As
	With old KE	66 As
	With archaic KE	67 As
	With indetermined KE	68 As

LATIN INSCRIPTIONS

Series 17	With MVNICI EMPORIA	69 As
Series 18	With QVAIS	
	Without QVAIS	70 As
	With countermark QVAIS	71 As
	With QVAIS on die	72 As
Series 19	Magistrates with two names	
	C.I.L.C. inscription in bracket	73 As
	curved inscription	74 As
	P.L.L.L. straight wings	75 As
	curved wings	76 As
	Smaller denominations, without magistrates names	
	EM-P	77 Sextans
	EM	78 Sextans
	IM	79 Sextans
	indeterminate	77 to 79 Sextans
	L.C.C.R.	80 As
Series 20	Without magistrates names, curved wings	
	MP without ligature	81 As
	MP with ligature	82 As

Series 21	Magistrates with three names	
	P.I.P.C.S.M.	
	MP with ligature	83 As
	without ligature	84 As
	C.I.NICOM - P.FL	85 As
	C.I.NICOM - P.FL/P.FL.Q	86 As
	Smaller denominations without magistrates names	87 Sextans
	C.P.C.M.S.R.	88 As
Series 22	With only one magistrate	
	L.M.RVF.P.C.Q.	89 As
Series 23	End of the former style	
	M.O.L.A.	90 As
	M.O.H.L.A.F.	91 As
	M.O.H.L.A.F. unusual wings	92 As
	P.C.PV.Q.C.C.	93 As
Series 24	New style, with magistrates of three names	
	C.S.B.L.C.M.	94 As
	CN.C.P.C.M.A. with Q beneath head	95 As
	CN.C.P.C.M.A. with CN beneath head	96 As
	CN.C.GR.L.C.F.	97 As
	CN.C.GR.L.C.FA.	98 As
	C.CA.T.C.O.CA	99 As
	C.CA.T.C.C.CAR	100 As
	C.T.C.Q.C.CA	101 As
	C.O.C.C.M.A. with Q beneath head	102 As
	C.O.C.C.M.A. with Q before head	103 As
	M.A.B.M.F. (M) with Q beneath head	104 As
	M.A.B.M.F. with M.Q behind head	105 As
	M.A.B.M.F.M. with Q behind head	106 As
Series 25	Without names of magistrates	
	Pallas with small head	107 As
	Smaller denominations	108 Quadrans
	Pallas with large head	109 As
Series 26	Countermarked coins with D.D. and dolphin	
	On coins no. 107	110 As
	On coins no. 109	111 As

Irregular positions of countermarks

    a) dolphin on obverse
    b) D.D. on obverse
    c) D.D. on reverse
    d) D.D. on obverse and reverse
    e) D.D. and dolphin on obverse, and D.D. on reverse
    f) D.D. and dolphin on obverse and dolphin on reverse

Series 27	Other countermarks	
	two palms	113 As
	eagle's head	114 As
	sword	115 As
	herring-bone	116 As
	N	117 As
	NIO	118 As
	IMI.BT	119 As
	NVMEL	120 As
	MPM	121 As
Series 28	Smaller denominations with VL	122 Quadrans

SERIES 1

1. As. O/Pallas, round helmet. R/Pegasus-Kabeirus, I.2. Mod. 31
   V.XIII-3, H.II-1, V.72 1.

	Weight (g)	Die Axis		Weight (g)	Die Axis
MAB 244	27.96	3	MAN 2874	21.14	10
MAB 314	24.26	2	MAN 2875	20.20	11
MAB 541	11.29 (halved)	6	Glasgow 963	25.38	-
			Mainz = H.II-1	26.70	-
MAB 615	27.92	3	Barril	-	-
MAB 1498	23.23	1	Ferrer	24	0
GNC 33603	30.30	0	Ferrer	20.30	7
*M Vic	-	-	Pellicer	27	3
MAN 2869	26.46	2	Riera	23.88	7
MAN 2870	23.88	11	Villoldo	21.60	7
MAN 2873	22.80	6	MAB 2871	25.00	4

2. Semis. O/Pallas, round helmet. R/Bull, I.2. Mod. 25
   V.XIV-1, V.72 1a1.

MAB 1137	12.07	5	Guerin	-	-
Almirall	11.14	3	Guadan 4840	8.70	0
*Balsach	12.10	6	Tizón	10.50	5
Balsach	9.12	7	Tizón	11	7
Ferrer	10	3	Vilaret	13.80	6
Grau	10.50	3	Villaronga 1837	9.75	6
			Villaronga 1838	9.40	11

3. Semis. O/Pallas, round helmet, before I.11. R/Bull, I.2. Mod. 24
   V.XIV-7, V.72 1a2.

MAB 215	13.13	6	Almirall	9.65	5
MAB 623	14.62	9	Badia	8.35	6
*GNC 13806	12.02	10	Guadán 1428	11.30	3
Sub. ANE 1963-			Guerin	-	-
no. 83	9.70	-	Grau	9.50	2
Romagosa	9.27	-	Villaronga 3708	13.60	4

4. Sextans. O/Pallas, round helmet, before I.15. R/Horse galloping,
   I.2. Mod. 15.
   V.XIV-3, V.72 1c.

GNC 13803	4.49	4	Villaronga 186	4.95	2
Baucis	4.55	6	*Villoldo	4.13	10

5. As. O/Pallas, round helmet. R/Pegasus-Kabeirus, I.2, wreath above
   croup. Mod. 31.
   V. 72 2.

MAB 221	25.03	2	Casas	21.40	-
MAB 542	12.04	4	Grau	21.50	7
	(halved)		Guadán 286	19.90	11
MAB 1056	21.63	-	Guadán 4444	25.50	0
MAB 1265	18.77	9	Guerin	26.50	0
MAB 1496	25.24	3	Oriola	21.10	-
MAB 1554	18.98	9	Pagés	21.20	4
MAB 2872	23.22	6	Pagés	19.30	0
Sub.ANE 1959-	26.05	-	Tizón	21.45	11
no. 202			Tizón	18.60	9
Aldecoa	21.50	10	Villaronga 936	24.95	3
Andorra	22.70	2	Villaronga 1819	21.75	10
Baucis	23.70	1	*Villoldo	26.60	10

6. Semis. O/Pallas, round helmet, I.11. R/Bull, I.2, wreath above croup.
   Mod. 23.
   V.XIV-10, V.72 2al.

MAB 23	11.40	11	MAN 2917	12.07	5
MAB 24	11.83	9	MAN 2918	9.36	11
MAB 208	10.26	0	MAN 2919	6.34	5
MAB 392	8.40	2	Sub. ANE 1963-	10.60	-
MAB 923	12.56	4	no. 84		
MAB 1124	9.52	-	Almirall	10.95	2
MAB 1452	10.56	-	*Guadán 4839	7.75	12
MAN 2916	12.60	7			

7. Quadrans. O/Pallas, round helmet, I.12. R/Lion, I.2, above wreath.
   Mod. 20.
   V.XIV-2 (without mark), V.72. 2bl.

MAB 12	4.22	3	BM 65	6.39	2
MAB 13	4.79	12	München SNG 102	6.04	6
MAB 14	6.06	5	Almirall	6.35	7
MAB 247	5.64	1	Almirall	4.95	2
MAB 328	8.25	2	Baucis	8.60	4
MAB 370	5.60	-	Baucis	7.50	9
MAB 445	5.35	-	Guadán 4848	6.25	11
MAB 529	5.26	11	Nuix	3.96	10
MAB 593	4.35	3	Padrones	4.80	6
MAT 1826	7.82	3	Romagosa	7.38	-
*M Vic	-	-	Vilaret	5.50	10
MAN 2879	6.56	10	Villaronga 1840	5.15	6

8. Sextans. O/Pallas, round helmet, I.15. R/Horse galloping, I.2, above
wreath, Mod. 17.
V.XV-3, V.72 2c.

MAB 207	3.82	6	Almirall	4.80	5
MAB 1141	4.27	6	Badia	-	6
MAB 1192	2.62	6	Balsach 6369	3.90	3
MAN 2880	4.49	6	Baucis	3.85	6
* BM 68	7.33	12	Guadán 309	4.20	9
MAB 928	4.44	4	Pellicer	4.21	10

9. Semis. O/Pallas, round helmet, I.11. R/Bull, I.2, above crecent, in
exergue dolphin. Mod. 22.
V.XIV-9 and 11 (worse description), V.72 2a2.

MAB 19	7.43	5	Grau	9.63	2
*MAN 2925	8.54	2	Villaronga 380	7.77	2
Paris, Luynes	8.31	2	Villaronga 2198	7.65	5
Andorra	4.48	1			

10. Quadrans. O/Pallas, round helmet, I.12. R/Lion I.2, above wreath,
beneath cornucopiae. Mod. 172.
V.XV-2, V.72 2b2.

GNC 33653	3.94	5	Almirall	5.75	6
MAN 2921	4.32	11	Andorra	4.00	5
Berlin	-	-	Badia	3.25	7
BM 66	3.89	12	Baucis	3.16	10
Paris, Luynes	4.01	11	Baucis	3.80	11
Sub. ANE 1963 no. 87	5.60	-	Guadán 205	3.00	12
			*Riera	3.85	12
			Villaronga 1057	4.40	11

SERIES 2

11. As. O/Pallas, helmet with two lobules. R/Pegasus-Kabeirus, I.2.
Mod. 31.
V.XIII-8, V.72 3.

MAB 906	22.31	5	Aldecoa	19.20	6
MAT 1830	21.84	11	Almirall	21.35	4
M Puig	-	-	Rectoret	17.80	9
* Andorra	24.10	2	Col. particular	26.00	3
			Col. particular	-	9

12. As. O/Pallas, helmet with two lobules. R/Pegasus-Kabeirus, I.2,
wreath above croup. Mod. 31.
V.XIII-4, V.72 4.

MAB 27	21.97	11	Corpus Christi 3	20.96	12
MAB 204	23.12	2	Paris, Luynes 56	23.23	1
MAB 211	19.83	12	M Puig	21.50	11

MAB 251	10.15 (halved)	9	M. Puig	20.50	4
			M. Puig	20.00	2
MAB 258	22.96	12	*Almirall	21.03	12
MAB 616	21.74	12	Guadán 289	22.50	11
MAB 1109	23.34	3	Pellicer	21.40	12
MAB 1255	21.31	11	Riera	27.42	5
Corpus Christi 2	19.98	7			

13. As. O/Pallas, helmet with two lobules, I.7, R/Pegasus-Kabeirus, I.2, wreath above croup. Mod. 32.
    V. XIV-4, H.II-2, V.72 5.

MAB 210	22.22	9	Badia	18.70	2
MAB 380	17.99	2	Cardim	22.65	7
MAB 654	17.41	2	Guadán 4826	24.50	9
MAB 1157	25.32	6	Guadán 4829	16.65	3
*MAN 2885	25.39	2	Guercin	-	-
MAN 2886	21.11	6	Pellicer	24.70	9
MAN 2887	18.40	5	Tizón	19.00	9
MAN 2888	15.62	5	Villaronga 1054	20.30	4
M. Puig	18.25	-	Villaronga 1449	21.65	6
M. Puig	17.50	-			

14. Quadrans. O/Pallas, helmet with two lobules, I.12. R/Lion, I.2, wreath above croup. Mod. 19.
    V.XV-1, V.72 5b.

GNC 13843	5.60	9	Sub. ANE 1963	5.05	-
MAN 2920	4.80	9	no. 85		
M Puig	6.20	1	Ferrer	4.50	6
M Puig	3.50	2	Ferrer	7.40	7
M Puig	2.50	3	*Villaronga 151	6.15	2
			Villoldo	4.85	2

SERIES 3

15. As. O/Pallas, I.1. R/Pegasus-Kabeirus, I.6. Mod. 30.
    V.XVI-8, H.II-7, V.72-6.

MAB 212	22.39	9	Baucis	28.00	2
MAB 907	27.81	6	Vidal	19.90	6
MAB 968	25.40	3	Villaronga 1059	26.05	4
MAB 969	26.73	12	Villoldo	26.00	6
MAB 1360	18.30	9	Villoldo	22.65	6
M Puig	19.80	6	*Villoldo	17.90	12

16. Semis. O/Pallas, I. 1. R/Bull, I.10. Mod 24.
    V.XVI-10, H.II-6, V.72 6a.

MAB 20	12.41	2
MAB 209	9.51	3

MAB 296	12.45	11	Andorra	11.55	5
MAB 373	9.01	2	Andorra	10.05	4
MAB 924	9.89	3	Baucis	12.35	11
MAB 1127	9.22	9	Baucis	13.55	10
MAB 1197	13.06	3	Baucis	9.30	5
MAB 1493	13.53	-	Baucis	10.70	5
A * GNC 13805	11.86	11	Baucis	11.95	2
M Vic	6.80	9	Cardim	10.73	10
M Vic	-	-	Ferrer	11.50	9
M Puig	-	-	Ferrer	5.80	10
M Puig	11.50	11	Guadán 307	13.80	6
MAN 2931	12.48	12	Guadán 4844	10.80	6
MAN 2932	9.65	3	Guerin	-	-
MAN 2933	8.35	3	Nuix	11.38	9
MAN 2934	8.17	5	Riera	10.60	7
MAN 2935	7.56	7	Tizón	10.45	9
MAN 2936	6.69	-	Vall	-	-
BM 70	14.99	3	Víctor Catalá 264	10.48	-
BM 71	13.16	3			
BM 72	12.59	3	Víctor Catalá 269	8.77	-
Gotha	-	-			
Mainz, Haeberlin 128	12.43	-	Villaronga 317	12.25	3
München SNG 101	10.67	5	Villaronga 1058	13.25	6
Sub ANE 1959 no. 232	8.35	-	Villaronga 1824	12.65	3
Sub ANE 1963 no. 97	10.00	-	Villaronga 1825	12.85	9
Sub ANE 1963 no. 98	12.70	-	Villoldo	15.60	2
Sub ANE 1969 no. 42	-	-	B * Villoldo	11.13	6
Almirall	11.00	9	Villoldo	10.00	1
Almirall	15.05	6	Vincke I-1	-	-
Andorra	11.50	6	Vincke I-2	-	-
			Col. part.	10.30	11

17. Quadrans. O/Pallas, I.1. R/Lion, I.12. Mod. 19.
    V.XVI-12, H.II-4, V.72 6b.

MAB 220	5.12	5	Baucis	5.70	11
MAB 346	3.21	9	Baucis	4.75	7
MAB 1404	4.66	-	Baucis	4.20	3
MAN 2943	4.48	6	Guerin	-	-
MAN 2944	3.44	5	Víctor Catalá 282	5.62	-
BM 67=H.II-4	5.44	3	Víctor Catalá 283	5.52	-
BM 69	4.06	2	Víctor Catalá 284	5.43	-
Sub ANE 1963 no. 100	5.50	-	Víctor Catalá 285	5.32	-
Sub ANE 1963 no. 46	6.30	4	Víctor Catalá 286	5.08	-
Sub ANE 1965 no. 47	5.60	12	Víctor Catalá 292	3.77	-
A * Almirall	4.80	7	Víctor Catalá 293	3.52	-
Almirall	5.05	3	Vilaret	4.65	6
Andorra	3.70	10	B * Villaronga 1060	2.85	11
Balsach 5035	8.90	12			
Balsach 5037	3.80	12	Villaronga 1827	5.50	12
Baucis	6.15	12	Villoldo	6.42	8

Sub. ANE 1963 n 101	4.50	-	Villoldo	3.85	12
			Vincke II-7	-	-

18. Sextans. O/Pallas, I.1. R/Horse head, I.13 and two pellets. Mod. 14.
      V. XVI-14, H. II-10, V. 72 6c.

* M Puig	2.70	9	Baucis	3.45	6
IVDJ=V.XVI-14=	-	-	Guadán 4851	3.20	4
H.II-10			Vidal	3.20	7
BM 75	1.96	7	Villaronga 1061	3.30	6
Almirall	2.65	12	Villoldo	2.50	3
Andorra	2.52	6			

SERIES 4

19. Unit. O/Pallas, I.1. R/Lion running with the head low, I.8. MOD 25/27.
      V.XVI-6, H.II-5, V.72 7. now divided in no. 19 and 20.

MAB 280	13.74	6	Baucis	12.40	9
MAB 648	7.87	6	A*Baucis	11.10	11
	(halved)		Baucis	7.35	3
GNC 33644	12.37	5	Baucis	7.00	3
MAN 2926	16.45	3	Guadán 305	10.50	6
MAN 2927	14.09	7	B * Guadán 4843	10.95	3
MAN 2928	11.26	7	Guerin	16.70	10
MAN 2929	10.73	7	Guerin	16.40	12
Copenhage=Hill II-5	10.35	-	Villaronga 2061	10.70	12
Sub ANE 1973 no. 79	11.75	-	Vincke II-8	-	-
Almirall	13.05	12	Vincke II-9	-	-
Andorra	12.50	5	Col. part.	15.00	8
Baucis	7.00	10			
	(halved)				

20. Unit. O/Pallas, I.1. R/Lion, walking, with head raised, I.9. All the
      coins are of the same reverse die, and probably the obverse too.
      V.XVI-7, V.72-7. Mod. 25/27.

MAB 31	14.93	9	*MAB 911	20.16	12
MAB 400	12.00	-	MAB 2930	13.42	1
MAB 848	12.42	12			

21. Unit. O/Pallas, I.1. R/Lion, I.6. Mod. 25.

*GNC 30159	11.66	9

22. Half. O/Pallas, I.1. R/Seahorse, I.10. Mod. 21.
      V.XVI-11, H.II-9, V.72 7a

MAB 18	5.57	4	MAB 804	7.69	3
A*MAB 216	5.90	11	B*MAB 925	7.35	3
MAB 301	7.89	3	MAB 1196	5.45	3
MAB 331	5.28	12	MAB 1267	6.60	12
MAB 576	6.20	10	MAB 1402	5.48	-

MAB 1442	5.65	-	Baucis	6.40	8
MAB 1483	6.91	-	Baucis	4.70	7
MAB 1484	4.59	3	Guadán 308	6.40	12
MAB 1567	6.68	3	Guadán 4845	4.55	6
M Puig	-	-	Guerin	7.00	9
MAN 2937	8.42	4	Guerin	-	-
MAN 2938	8.25	9	Víctor Catalá 276	9.28	-
MAN 2939	7.68	9	Víctor Catalá 277	7.43	-
MAN 2940	5.87	9	Víctor Catalá 278	6.37	-
BM 73	7.60	2	Víctor Catalá 279	5.56	-
C*Copenhagen=H.II-9	5.95	-	Vidal	8.20	7
Paris, Luynes 82	4.86	5	Vidal	5.45	9
Sub ANE 1963 no. 99	4.60	-	Villaronga 159	5.05	8
Almirall	6.20	6	Villaronga 1826	8.45	2
Almirall	5.65	2	Villoldo	6.52	12
Badía	9.45	9	Villoldo	6.20	8
Balsach 5048	8.20	11	Vincke I-3	-	-
Baucis	7.80	5			
Baucis	6.80	2			

23. Fourth. O/Pallas, I.1. R/Cock, I.12. Mod. 17.
    V.XVI-13, H.II-11, V.72 7b.

MAB 15	3.03	6	Almirall	3.08	9
MAB 273	3.73	9	Andorra	4.58	2
MAB 366	2.78	-	Baucis	3.62	2
MAB 610	2.40	9	A*Baucis	2.25	10
MAB 756	5.09	8	Guadán 159	3.25	12
MAB 926	2.94	9	Guadán 160	3.10	5
MAB 927	2.90	3	Romagosa	3.55	-
GNC 13812	3.77	7	Tizón	2.80	6
M Puig	2.50	4	Víctor Catalá 296	3.72	-
MAN 2945	4.35	2	Víctor Catalá 297	3.39	-
MAN 2946	4.14	7	Víctor Catalá 298	3.19	-
MAN 2947	2.26	3	Víctor Catalá 299	2.67	-
Newell=H.II-11	3.54	-	Víctor Catalá 300	2.58	-
Sub ANE 1959 no. 236	2.70	-	Vidal	4.02	9
Sub ANE 1963 no. 102	2.85	-	B*Vilaret	3.10	7
Sub ANE 1963 no. 103	3.25	-	Villaronga 256	3.80	2
Sub ANE 1965 no. 48	2.95	-	Villaronga 1828	3.45	6
Sub ANE 1965 no. 49	3.55	-	Villoldo	3.65	2

24. Sixth. O/Pallas, I.1. R/Wild boar, I.14. Mod. 12.
    V.XVI-15, V.72 7c.

Sub ANE 1959 no. 238	1.00	-
*Baucis	1.20	11
Vilaret	4.05	3

SERIES 5

25. As. O/Pallas, I.7. R/Pegasus-Kabeirus, I.2. wreath above croup, small bull butting the pegasus. Mod. 31/32.
V.XIV-6, V.72 8.

MAB 293	20.23	11	*Balsach 5051	21.39	6
Azaila 690	20.75	8	Baucis	21.20	3
GNC 13873	19.66	3	Baucis	8.75	12
MAN 2881	27.45	9		(halved)	
MAN 2882	23.66	6	Guadán 292	19.30	11
MAN 2883	18.39	7	Riera	18.03	5
MAN 2884	17.65	10	Romagosa	18.27	-
MAT 2576	22.62	12	Tizón	23.15	7
MAT 2891	21.14	6	Tizón	20.90	2
BM 59	18.73	2	Tizón	18.20	7
BM 60	15.40	12	Vidal	22.30	11
Sub ANE 1959 no. 214	18.20	-	Vilaret	24.30	12
Sub ANE 1963 no. 82	23.00	-	Villaronga 185	19.40	8
M Puig	21.00	6	Villaronga 257	21.25	9
M Puig	20.00	3	Villaronga 3781	23.80	6
M Puig	19.50	11	Villoldo	22.30	9
M Puig	18.00	2	Col part.	23.90	10
Aldecoa	21.50	9	Col part.	-	-
Almirall	20.12	12			
Almirall	19.51	5			

26. ?. O/Pallas, I.7 and I.20, prow behind the neck. R/Pegasus-Kabeirus, I.2, wreath above croup, small bull butting the pegasus. All the coins are from the same dies. Mod. 29.
V.XV-8, V.72 8b.

MAB 829	10.39	3	Sub Circulo	10.20	8
A * HSA	11.30	3	VI-72 no. 3		
			B * Tizón	8.70	9

SERIES 6

27. As. O/Pallas, helmet with two lobules. R/Pegasus-Kabeirus, I.3. Mod. 32.
V.72 9

MAB 203	24.74	9	MAB 1268	21.27	11
* MAB 269	17.36	2	M Vic	-	-
MAB 453	20.84	8	M Vic	-	-
MAB 480	19.39	5	Andorra	18.92	7
MAB 1158	20.07	5	Grau	16.00	6
			Villaronga 1820	16.50	5

27 bis. As. O/Pallas, helmet with two lobules. R/Pegasus-Kabeirus, I.3, wreath above croup, in exergue caduceus left. Mod. 31. V.XIII-5.

M. Prado, Madrid   -   -

28. As. O/Pallas, helmet with two lobules. R/Pegasus-Kabeirus, I.3, palm to right of the inscription, in exergue winged caduceus right. Mod. 31. V.72 11

Pujol y Camps 112	19.13	-			
*Villoldo	18.10	6	Col. part.	18.80	5

29. As. O/Pallas, helmet with two lobules. R/Pegasus-Kabeirus, I.4, in exergue caduceus right. Mod. 31. V.XIII-7, V.72 10A.

* BM 58	12.53	3	Baucis	17.50	8
Stockholm	17.32	-	Domenech	17.00	4
Sub ANE 1963 no. 75	20.10	-	Tizón	25.10	1
Almirall	19.67	2	Villaronga 667	18.20	8
Andorra	23.05	8	Villaronga 1052	18.35	5

30. As. O/Pallas, helmet with two lobules. R/Pegasus-Kabeirus, I.4, in exergue caduceus left. Mod. 31. V.XIII-6, V.72 10B.

MAB 205	19.85	6	MAN 2908	12.02	3
M Puig	20.50	9	Tizón	19.02	7
M Puig	19.50	11	Vilaret	18.00	9
MAN 2905	18.75	11	Villaronga 1492	19.10	9
MAN 2906	16.85	11	*Villoldo	21.45	2
MAN 2907	16.54	11	Villoldo	19.50	2

31. As. O/Pallas. R/Pegasus-Kabeirus, I.4, wreath before. Mod. 30. V.72 12, 13.

A * MAB 791	19.45	4	B * M Puig	16.00	11
MAB 1044	21.74	6	M Puig	13.00	11
MAB 1489	12.39	6	C * Aldecoa	22.90	7
MAT 2646	20.60	4	Almirall	22.90	9
M Puig	22.50	5	Pellicer	15.30	3

32. Semis. O/Pallas. R/Bull, I.3. Mod. 19/21. V.72 12a.

MAB 708	7.59	2	A * Almirall	6.41	12
MAB 1438	8.22	-	Almirall	5.20	77
MAB 1406	6.95	-	Andorra	6.35	9
Aldecoa	4.95	2	Guerin	-	-
Almirall	7.85	11	B * Villaronga 3084	6.02	10

SERIES 7

33. As.   O/Pallas, I.16.   R/Pegasus-Kabeirus, I.3, beneath I.17, and
    above pegasus I.21.   Mod. 28.
    V.XVI-1, V.72 14.

* Paris 69	25.35	6
Víctor Catalá	20.41	12
Villaronga 712	16.05	3

34. Semis.   O/Pallas, short I.17.   R/Bull, I.3, above I.16.   Mod. 20.
    V.XVI-2, V.72 14a.

GNC 33632	8.07	3
* HSA 12194	4.96	12
Sub ANE 1963 no. 95	6.05	-

35. Quadrans.   O/Pallas, short I.17.   R/Lion, I.3, above I.16.   Mod. 15.
    V.XVI-3, V.72 14b.

* M del Prado	-	-

36. Semis.   O/Pallas, I.18.   R/Bull, I.3, above I.19.   Mod. 22.
    V.XVI-4, H.II-8, V.72 15a1.

MAN 2941	11.45	5	Baucis	6.35	6
MAN 2942	7.75	5	Domenech	8.80	12
BM 74	5.92	12	Guadán 4841	8.25	7
Paris=I.II-8	7.93	-	Pellicen	6.15	3
Sub ANE 1959 no. 228	8.20	-	Villaronga 267	4.98	2
Almirall	7.47	8	* Villaronga 1818	7.90	9
Barril	-	-	Villaronga 300	8.50	8

37. Quadrans.   O/Pallas, I.18.   R/Lion, I.3, above I.19.   Mod. 16.
    V.XVI-5, V.72 15b.

MAB 518	2.05	9	* M Puig	4.00	12
MAB 602	2.71	3	Sub ANE 1963	5.40	-
MAB 747	3.42	11	no. 96		
MAB 1311	5.72	-	Balsach 5038	3.35	6
GNC 33651	3.75	3	Guadán 4846	3.65	3
M Vic	-	7	Víctor Catalá 290	3.93	-
			Víctor Catalá 291	3.81	-

38. Semis.   O/Pallas, I.11.   R/Bull, I.3, above I.19.   Mod. 20.
    V.72 15a2.

* GNC 30136	8.18	2	Romagosa	6.00	9

SERIES 8

39. As. O/Pallas. I.7. R/Pegasus-Kabeirus, I.3, wreath before. Mod. 30/31.
    V.XIV-5, V.72 16.

MAB 29	20.07	12	Baucis	22.65	12
MAB 1170	16.82	12	Baucis	21.90	8
MAB 1175	-	12	Baucis	20.55	2
MAB 1261	29.86	6	Baucis	17.50	7
MAB 1345	20.88	6	Cullell	20.00	6
MAB 1531	19.08	2	Domenech	20.60	1
MAB 1532	18.91	9	Ferrer	19.20	6
MAB 1533	23.09	2	Grau	22.02	7
MAB 1534	23.24	12	Guadán 291	20.90	6
MAB 1535	21.89	11	Guadán 4827	22.80	8
MAB 1536	21.31	1	Guadán 4828	28.45	11
MAB 1537	22.42	7	Guadán 4830	24.55	11
MAB 1538	20.46	2	Guadán 4831	19.70	6
MAB 1539	21.15	6	Guerin	20.75	8
MAB 1540	22.44	6	Guerin	-	-
MAB 1541	21.01	12	Pagés	24.20	2
MAB 1542	24.00	6	Riera	21.10	7
MAB 1543	23.90	2	A*Riera	20.39	1
MAB 1544	20.54	4	Riera	20.20	5
MAB 1545	19.53	2	Riera	17.65	11
IEI	-	-	Serra	20.30	3
M Mataró	20.60	-	Vidal	19.10	11
M Puig	-	-	Vidal	20.30	11
M Puig	-	-	Vilaret	-	-
BM 63	21.36	11	Villaronga 278	21.30	4
BM 64	23.98	6	B*Villaronga	21.50	10
M Milano	-	-	1817		
Sub ANE 1963 no. 74	18.60	-	Villaronga 1836	20.05	4
Sub ANE 1963 no. 81	21.40	-	Villaronga 2741	18.30	11
Almirall	25.85	5	Villoldo	21.00	7
Almirall	23.40	4	Villoldo	21.40	3
Almirall	22.30	6	Vincke II-5	-	-
Almirall	21.10	2	Col part.	-	-
Almirall	20.25	7	Col part.	22.10	5
Almirall	20.20	3	Col part.	19.20	3
Andorra	19.05	9	Col part.	22.10	10
Andorra	18.75	5			
Andorra	18.60	7			
Andorra	18.50	4			

40. Semis. O/Pallas, I.11. R/Bull, above crescent, I.3. Mod. 22.
    V.XIV-8, V.72 16a.

MAB 32	10.97	11	MAB 827	5.48	11
MAB 595	5.20	12	MAB 1530	9.32	6

MAT 2661	10.24	6	*Almirall	10.70	3
M Banyoles	10.50	11	Cullell	5.00	3
M Banyoles	8.27	6	Ferrer	6.00	5
			Tizón	8.70	6

41. Quadrans. O/Pallas, I.12. R/Lion, above wreath, I.3. **Mod. 14.**
    V.72 16b.

MAB 342	3.08	12
Guadán 4847	2.20	9
*Villaronga 1842	2.45	9

SERIES 9

42. As. O/Pallas, I.7, behind jug. R/Pegasus-Kabeirus, wreath before, I.3, palm to right of the inscription. Mod. 30/31.
    V.XV-4, V.72 17.

MAB 28	24.48	10	Azaila 689	23.32	11
MAB 213	22.36	9	M Banyoles	27.65	9
MAB 417	16.79	11	M Banyoles	24.07	9
MAB 665	21.11	10	M Banyoles	20.50	2
MAB 1173	22.21	8	M Ibiza	19.40	12
MAB 1256	27.71	7	MAN 2899	22.87	12
MAB 1257	16.37	6	MAN 2900	21.82	6
MAB 1337	21.03	12	MAN 2901	20.92	7
MAB 1338	17.94	4	MAN 2902	20.05	2
MAB 1492	22.76	4	MAN 2903	17.37	1
MAB 1508	19.93	4	M Puig	-	-
MAB 1509	22.46	7	M. Puig	-	-
MAB 1510	19.49	9	B*M Puig 507	-	-
MAB 1511	28.81	2	M Puig	15.50	10
MAB 1512	20.74	9	BM 61	27.08	11
MAB 1513	17.60	9	BM 62	21.90	11
MAB 1514	27.40	3	Milano	-	-
MAB 1515	30.09	8	SNG München	25.61	7
MAB 1516	21.98	2	103		
MAB 1517	20.05	4	Paris, Luynes	21.96	4
MAB 1518	20.33	12	Sub ANE 1963	23.55	-
MAB 1519	24.42	6	Sub ANE 1968	20.80	-
MAB 1520	23.50	7	no. 40		
MAB 1521	18.50	5	Almirall	27.85	7
MAB 1522	19.39	3	Almirall	23.85	6
MAB 1523	20.31	5	Badia	16.38	2
MAB 1524	18.18	1	Balsach 5047	18.03	11
MAB 1525	21.12	8	Balsach 5049	18.00	12
MAB 1526	25.55	4	Barril	-	-
MAB 1527	23.24	2	Baucis	19.35	10
A*MAB 1528	22.32	1	Baucis	19.35	3
MAB 1551	22.63	-	Baucis	10.25	7

Domenech	-	-	Riera	22.60	10
Ferrer	20.00	12	Vall	-	-
Ferrer	16.90	12	Víctor Catalá 230	20.49	-
Grau	22.00	9			
Guadán 287	20.00	9	Víctor Catalá 236	19.28	-
Guadán 293	26.80	1			
Guadán 294	18.50	10	Vilaret	23.55	9
Guadán 295	18.90	3	Vilaret	21.40	10
Guerin	26.00	9	Villaronga 748	16.45	10
Guerin	14.70	12	Villaronga 1103	18.45	2
Guerin	19.30	9	Villaronga 3000	12.20	2
Orriols	18.30	10	Villaronga 3001	21.40	11
C * Pagés	20.15	11	D*Villoldo	29.80	5
Pellicer	22.30	11	Vincke II-6	-	-
Rectoret	20.70	12	Col part.	23.40	5
			Col part.	20.60	12
			Col. part	-	-
			Col part.	-	5

43. Semis. O/Pallas, behind jug. R/Bull, above crescent, I.3. Mod. 22.
    V.XV-5, V.72 17a.

MAB 16	9.94	11	*Baucis	4.95	6
MAB 1401	8.59	-	Espuny	8.80	3
MAB 1463	7.21	9	Gudán 4842	6.85	2
MAB 1529	8.75	6	Víctor Catalá 273	6.09	-
MAT 901	11.07	12	Vilaret	11.55	2
Almirall	9.20	3	Villaronga 158	6.60	11
			Villaronga 1841	12.60	9

44. Quadrans. O/Pallas, behind jug. R/Lion, above wreath, I.3. Mod.15.
    V.XV-6, V.72 17b.

MAB 1245	2.91	-	*Sub ANE 1963 no. 90	3.50	-

45. As. O/Pallas, behind jug, I.22. R/Pegasus-Kabeirus, wreath before,
    I.3. Mod. 31.
    V.XV-7, H.II-3, V.72 18.

MAB 292	23.41	8	*M Puig	21.10	2
MAB 1062	20.60	-	MAN 2904	18.69	3
MAB 1070	10.08 (halved)	-	SNG München 104	21.54	12
M Banyoles	-	-	Paris 68	21.68	11
M Mataró	28.60	2	Stockholm=Hill-II.3	24.17	-
			Domenech	14.60	2
			Villoldo	19.20	11

SERIES 10

46. As. O/Pallas, I.7. R/Pegasus-Kabeirus, wreath before, I.4, palm to right of the inscription. Mod. 30.
    V.72-19.

MAB 620	17.91	2	Villoldo	14.00	8
A*Villaronga 205	16.20	10	B*Villoldo,	15.15	11
Villaronga 206	16.25	2	grafiti I.23		
Baucis	17.60	8			

SERIES 11

47. As. O/Pallas, I.7. R/Pegasus-Kabeirus, I.4, wreath above croup, palm to right of the inscription. Mod. 30.
    V.72-20.

MAT 2561	11.83	10	Guerin	19.10	10
M Mataró	16.80	4	Nuix	14.30	9
Badia	16.55	6	Tizón	17.00	7
*Baucis	16.15	7	Villaronga 1821	24.70	2
Baucis	12.60	5	Villaronga 2736	12.20	6
Guadan 3153	20.50	9	Villaronga 2875	16.40	6

48. As. O/Pallas, helmet with two lobules. R/Pegasus-Kabeirus, wing like fan. I.4. Mod. 28.
    V.XIII-1, V.72-21A.

M Vic	-	-	Almirall	12.75	11
Sub ANE 1963 no. 73	14.50	-	*Villoldo	17.80	4

49. As. O/Pallas, with straight visor. R/Pegasus-Kabeirus, I.4. Mod. 27/28.
    V.XV-10, V.72-21B.

MAB 21	12.54	11	Almirall	14.16	12
MAB 30	15.85	3	Espuny	13.30	11
MAB 1322	20.73	-	Grau	10.40	11
MAB 1329	20.81	6	Guadán 4832	16.55	12
*MAN 2876	17.15	8	Riera	16.00	6
MAN 2877	15.13	2	Romagosa	15.10	11
MAN 2878	12.97	3	Tizón	16.55	9
Sub ANE 1963 no. 76	20.55	-	Villaronga 1822	17.35	3
Almirall	20.70	11	Villaronga 1834	19.05	2
Almirall	18.20	3	Villaronga 2907	16.20	11
Almirall	14.70	5	Vincke II-4	-	-

50. Semis. O/Pallas. R/Bull, I.4. Mod. 21.

* GNC 33636	8.22	12

51. As. O/Pallas. R/Pegasus-Kabeirus, I.4, in exergue I.6.
    V.XVI-9.

GNC 4526	12.05	7	Delgado	18.83	-
*Botet i Sisó I,	-	-	CXXXV-200		
page LIV no. 3					

52. As. O/Pallas, R/Pegasus-Kabeirus, before prow, Greek Φ above croup.
    Mod. 29.

A * Roger Grau	14.90	-
B * Pellicer	11.80	9

SERIES 12

53. As. O/Pallas, round helmet with straight visor. R/Pegasus-Kabeirus,
    I.4, above Nike flying and before prow. Mod. 27/29.
    V.72-22A.

MAB 1283	14.47	6	Baucis	14.65	11
MAB 1323	17.86	-	Baucis	12.10	2
GNC 4519	16.00	5	Baucis	10.35	11
GNC 33620	17.11	9	Baucis	8.70	5
M Puig	16.00	-	Grau	12.13	11
M Puig	13.50	4	Guadán 299	17.10	1
BM 76	15.79	10	Guadán 4834	18.10	3
Paris, Luynes 67	14.93	12	Guerin	22.30	2
Sub ANE 1959 no. 223	12.70	-	A * Guerin	15.80	9
Almirall	14.17	12	Riera	14.40	2
Almirall	13.92	2	Riera	15.10	6
Andorra	16.38	11	Tizón	16.40	9
Andorra	6.75	11	B * Tizón	13.86	4
Badia	14.80	-	Villaronga 152	14.60	9
Badia	12.90	4	Villaronga 1493	15.20	-
Baucis	21.00	6	Villaronga 1833	16.00	6
Baucis	15.40	12	C * Villoldo	14.50	7
			Villoldo	15.10	9
			Col part.	15.50	12

54. As. O/Pallas, helmet with side crest. R/Pegasus-Kabeirus, above
    Nike flying and before prow. Mod. 27/28.
    V.72-22B.

MAB 202	13.24	10	B * BM 77	11.61	2
MAB 770	21.16	7	Almirall	18.20	10
MAB 1319	17.72	12	Andorra	10.15	6
MAB 1320	11.87	2	C * Barril	-	-
MAB 1321	17.08	5	Cullell	17.30	3
GNC 13819	16.16	3	Ferrer	10.80	3
A * M Puig	14.20	2	Guerin	-	-
M Puig	12.00	9	Riera	12.35	10
M Puig	8.00	12	Riera	11.85	11

Tizón	15.20	3	Villoldo	13.45	2
Villaronga 187	12.55	12	Col part.	12.70	2
Villaronga 1832	12.45	7			
) * Villoldo	16.35	11			

5. As. O/Pallas, helmet with large crest. R/Pegasus-Kabeirus above Nike flying, before prow. Mod. 28/30.
    V.XV-11, V.72-22C.

IAB 26	15.76	6	Almirall	16.70	5
IAB 607	11.85	6	Guadán 4833	22.50	1
IAB 909	19.56	11	Guerin	-	-
IAB 1399	10.94	-	Guerin	-	-
	(halved)		A * Riera	22.70	12
I Puig	18.70	12	Tizón	12.20	6
I Puig	13.50	4	Villaret	18.51	9
IAN 2909	17.34	11	B * Villaronga	14.60	6
IAN 2910	16.10	3	5241		

6. Semis. O/Pallas, helmet with large crest. R/Bull, I.4, above crescent. Mod. 22/23.
    V.72-22Ca.

IAB 1430	12.00	-	* Balsach 5036	9.22	3
I Banyoles	-	-	Vidal	9.20	11

7. As. O/Pallas. R/Pegasus-Kabeirus, above Nike flying, I.4. Mod. 28.

GNC 33622	11.32	12	Pujol y Camps	14.12	-
NC 33623	15.30	11	121		

8. As. O/Pallas, straight visor. R/Pegasus-Kabeirus, I.4, prow before pegasus. Mod. 29.
    V.XIII-2, V.72-23A.

NC 33617	15.67	6	Guadán 296	17.00	2
Almirall	16.90	3	Villaronga 1835	19.50	7

SERIES 13

9. As. O/Pallas, with side crest. R/Pegasus-Kabeirus, I.4, prow before pegasus. Mod. 25/26.
    V.72-23B.

IAB 1104	11.98	12	Badia	7.45	5
IAN 2911	14.31	4	A * Balsach 5785	17.15	7
IAN 2912	11.62	9	Baucis	10.00	10
IAN 2913	11.33	2	Cardim	11.10	11
IAN 2914	9.76	12	Ferrer	14.00	6
AN 2915	8.29	10	Guadán 206	9.10	7
NE 1965 no. 44	12.70	3	Guadán 306	9.80	6
uorra	12.68	11	B * Guadán 4837	12.15	5

Nuix	13.90	10	Villaronga 1053	15.95	5
Vidal	10.70	6	Villaronga 2074	9.50	12
Villaronga 750	14.85	8	Villoldo	11.50	5

60. As. O/Pallas left. R/Pegasus-Kabeirus, I.4, prow before pegasus.
    Mod. 27.
    V.XV-12, V.72-23C.

MAB 709	10.98	10	Baucis	11.20	6
* GNC 33618	11.24	11	Lizana	15.00	-
Stockholm	8.18	1			

SERIES 14

61. Semis. O/Pallas, round helmet, R/Bull, above crescent, I.4. Mod. 19/20.
    V.72-24a.

MAB 17	4.95	5	MAB 1569	3.49	12
MAB 710	12.05	5	GNC 14362	6.21	over-strike
MAB 1174	8.58	7	M Puig	8.50	4
MAB 1244	3.44	-	A * M Puig	-	-
MAB 1274	6.59	6	Andorra	5.95	7
MAB 1299	5.12	12	B * Balsach 5046	5.35	11
MAB 1403	-	-	Baucis	5.40	12
MAB 1407	6.90	-	Ferrer	5.20	7
MAB 1441	8.66	-	Grau	5.25	9
MAB 1461	6.78	9	Tizón	5.00	6
MAB 1464	3.75	9	C * Vidal	6.60	4
			Villaronga 1839	5.55	6

62. Semis. O/Pallas, helmet of two lobules. R/Bull, above crescent, I.4.
    Mod. 20.
    V.XV-9, V.72-13a.

MAB 297	5.88	2	Sub ANE 1956 no. 219		-
MAB 362	6.79	10	Aldecoa	6.00	2
MAB 983	5.66	-	Baucis	5.10	7
MAN 2922	5.89	2	Guadán 4849	3.65	9
A * MAN 2923	5.33	12	B * Villaronga	8.10	8
MAN 2924	4.70	4	1056		
			Villoldo	4.85	5

63. Semis. O/Pallas, helmet of two lobules. R/Bull, I.4, above crescent
    and Iberian letter A. Mod. 21.
    V.XIV-12.

* GNC 33635	7.30	3

SERIES 15

64. As. O/Pallas. R/Pegasus (normal head) I.4, above Nike flying, prow before pegasus. Mod. 25.
V.72-25.

Guadán 288	10.10	-	* Villaronga	9.35	11
Savès	-	-	2075		

SERIES 16

65. As. O/Pallas, I.7. R/Pegasus (normal head), wreath above croup, I.3 (the Iberian letters TI, generally have their ends parallel). Mod. 25/28.
V.XV-13, V.72-26A.

MAB 227	9.21	10	Cardim	9.70	7
MAB 594	11.53	9	Ferrer	14.70	9
MAB 825	13.88	6	Grau	12.27	9
MAB 828	11.18	11	Grau	-	12
MAB 908	13.50	6	Guerin	-	-
MAB 1129	11.02	6	Guadán 302	11.50	7
MAT 1853	11.71	-	Guadán 4835	11.05	12
M Puig	10.70	-	Guadán 4836	13.50	9
M Puig	-	-	B * Guerin	12.30	2
M Puig	-	-	Hillgarth	10.20	2
M Puig	-	-	Pellicer	11.60	6
Paris, Luynes 60	11.10	7	Riera	9.90	2
Sub ANE 1959 no. 221	12.35	-	Riera	9.26	4
Almirall	13.60	3	Tizón	12.90	11
Almirall	13.60	8	Villaronga 1830	13.75	3
Andorra	11.88	7	Villaronga 3002	11.20	5
Balsach	10.57	6	Villoldo	12.35	5
Barril	-	-	Villoldo	10.45	5
Baucis	11.90	4	Villoldo	10.12	7
Baucis	9.55	11	Col part.	-	6
Cardim	14.60	12			

66. As. O/Pallas, I.7. R/Pegasus (normal head), wreath above croup, I.2 (the Iberian letters TI generally have their ends parallel). Mod. 25/28.
V.72-26B.

MAB 334	8.58	11	Almirall	8.92	6
MAB 605	12.97	12	Almirall	14.30	12
MAB 1138	9.46	2	Naucis	12.80	7
MAN 2889	15.64	1	Baucis	12.80	8
MAN 2890	15.45	10	Baucis	12.20	4
M Vic	-	-	Cardim	13.15	3
M Puig	-	-	Grau	10.93	12
SNG München 106	9.03	3	Grau	10.27	4
Aldecoa	10.45	6	Guerin	12.90	7
Almirall	12.75	4	Guadán 304	8.50	7
			* Romagosa	11.70	3

67. As. O/Pallas, I.7. R/Pegasus (normal head), wreath above croup, I.5. Mod. 25/28.
V.72-26C.

MAB 206	10.81	3	Almirall	10.70	4
MAB 852	13.36	8	Andorra	12.35	7
MAB 910	11.66	3	Andorra	11.85	1
A * M Puig	-	-	Andorra	11.20	8
M Puig	-	-	Andorra	8.10	11
MAN 2891	12.97	6	Baucis	10.85	1
MAN 2893	10.06	4	Riera	10.45	5
MAN 2894	10.00	12	Tizón	8.85	3
MAN 2895	9,84	2	Tizón	7.45	5
MAN 2896	9.52	2	Vilaret	10.80	3
MAN 2897	9.52	2	Villaronga 214	10.00	9
MAN 2898	5.52	-	Villaronga 669	11.10	5
B * BM 78	12.86	7	Villaronga 841	9.65	12
BM 79	9.60	1	Villaronga 1055	19.40	7
Paris, Luynes 59	9.55	8	Villaronga 1823	10.15	12
Sub ANE 1965 no. 45	11.00	12	Villaronga 1831	9.90	12
Almirall	13.30	12	Villoldo	12.82	2
			Col part.	-	11

68. As. Uncertain coins corresponding to 65, 66 and 67, and not classified in them as not showing clearly the Iberian letter Ke. Mod. 25/28.

MAB 22	13.16	6	MAT 2201	6.19	6
MAB 238	8.90	5	MAT 3125	10.56	4
MAB 239	10.30	5	GNC 13857	12.33	10
MAB 333	4.97	3	M Eivissa	11.20	9
	(halved)		M Puig	12.95	-
MAB 403	14.47	5	M Puig	-	-
MAB 435	9.29	6	M Puig	-	-
MAB 578	5.22	7	M Puig	-	-
	(halved)		SNG München 105	13.20	7
MAN 649	5.82	9			
	(halved)		Aldecoa	7.30	6
MAB 847	9.04	11	Almirall	9.65	12
MAB 1010	6.58	7	Almirall	9.60	11
	(halved)		Almirall	8.53	5
MAB 1169	11.05	11	Grau	-	3
MAB 1183	10.50	11	Guerin	-	-
MAB 1260	8.76	7	Pellicer	14.30	11
MAB 1284	19.18	-	Pellicer	11.80	6
MAB 1292	8,76	11	Tizón	12.80	2
MAB 1400	5.62	-	Tizón	11.50	2
	(halved)		Tizón	9.00	1
MAB 1462	6.29	-	Vall	-	-
	(halved)		Vall	-	-
MAB 1489	-	7	Vilaret	12.32	12
MAB 1490	12.83	-	Vilaret	-	9

SERIES 17

69. As. O/Head of Artemis right with arrow and quiver, in front EMPORIA, sometimes right, sometimes circular. R/Pegasus right, beneath MUNICI. Mod. 25/26.
V.CXXI-1, H.III-1, V.64-5.

MAB 40	8.27	5	Balsach 5509	8.15	11
MAB 175	8.50	3	Balsach 5999	9.50	6
MAB 198	9.11	11	Baucis	11.76	6
MAB 201	11.46	1	Baucis	11.45	5
MAB 248	5.88	12	Baucis	9.96	3
	(halved)		Ferrer	8.50	12
MAB 254	9.21	6	Ferrer	8.50	7
MAB 426	10.17	7	Guadán 3145	12.30	5
MAB 630	10.04	5	Guadán 3146	12.00	7
MAB 919	16.05	12	Guadán 3147	13.00	5
MAB 1132	9.60	3	Guadán 4852	12.25	2
MAB 1134	10.50	12	Guerin	-	-
MAB 1262	9.12	-	Guerin	-	-
MAB 1279	9.28	2	Guerin	-	-
MAB 1466	-	3	Guerin	-	-
MAT 2560	11.84	4	Guerin	-	-
IVDJ	-	-	Pellicer	9.15	3
BM 80	11.00	11	Romagosa	6.30	12
BM 81	10.87	2	Sorjus	13.16	12
Aldecoa	9.40	8	Víctor Catalá 332	13.84	5
Almirall	12.20	2			
Almirall	10.80	7	A * Vilaret	16.25	7
Almirall	10.70	6	Villaronga 286	10.85	9
Almirall	9.95	3	Villaronga 596	10.25	2
Almirall	9.30	9	Villaronga 597	12.80	7
Almirall	5.79	9	Villaronga 1843	14.10	11
Andorra	10.78	5	B*Villaronga 1844	11.80	3
Andorra	9.70	8			
			Villoldo	12.27	10
			C*Villoldo	12.00	11

SERIES 18

70. As. O/Pallas. R/Pegasus, wreath above croup, beneath EMPORIT. Mod. 25.

A * BM	10.47	3	B * Tizón	8.40	6

71. As. O/Pallas, with countermark QVAIS. R/Pegasus, wreath above croup, beneath EMPORIT. Mod. 25.
V.64-1

A * Almirall	-	2	B * Guadán 3144	11.35	9
Guadán 297	6.60	9	Riera	8.50	3

72. As. O/Pallas, in front QVAIS. R/Pegasus, wreath above croup,
   beneath EMPORIT. Mod. 26.
   V.121-2, H. III-3, V.64-2

A * MAB 36	14.85	6	Balsach 6000	15.25	4
MAB 275	15.09	12	Balsach 5507	8.65	8
MAB 386	6.34	3	D * Balsach 5508	6.05	12
	(halved)		Baucis	16.12	9
MAB 663	10.03	2	Baucis	11.00	7
MAB 920	16.05	7	Baucis	7.20	12
MAB 1190	-	-		(halved)	
MAB 1280	9.24	3	Cullell	7.60	1
B * GNC	-	-	Ferrer	9.50	12
	(halved)		Guadán 4853	11.95	6
MAT 2566	12.76	4	E * Romagosa	11.30	2
C * M Puig	7.80	6	Tizón	12.00	3
BM 2186	11.80	2	Vidal	14.00	6
Wien 322	-	-	Vilaret	11.00	2
Almirall	13.14	2	Villaronga 1845	11.50	6
Almirall	11.95	12	Villaronga 2101	14.50	5
Almirall	9.55	10	Villoldo	10.30	12
Andorra	10.30	9	Villoldo	8.20	3
Andorra	10.00	7	Col part.	11.50	3

SERIES 19

73. As. O/Pallas, in front C.I.L.C.Q. R/Pegasus, wreath above croup,
   beneath EMPORIT on tablet. Mod. 25.
   V.121-3 and 8. V.64-3.

Pujol y Camps MNE III, p. 165 with countermark DD and dolphin.

MAB 686	5.75	9	Andorra	11.32	12
	(halved)		Barril	-	-
MAB 856	7.71	6	Baucis	11.50	11
MAB 877	3.32	4	Baucis	10.60	4
	(halved)		B * Baucis	9.96	12
MAB 878	3.62	3	Domenech	9.00	12
	(halved)		Guadán 2046	11.00	12
MAB 1037	12.18	11	Guerin	-	-
MAB 1355	-	11	de la Pinta	-	-
M Puig	-	-	Víctor Catalá 1.	-	-
A * BM 83	5.99	6	1.IV.1		
BM 84	15.78	6	Villaronga 153	9.35	2
Almirall	13.70	5	Villaronga 1847	9.20	9
Almirall	10.67	7	Villoldo	11.85	5
Almirall	9.20	4			

74. As. Similar to 73, but EMPORIT curved. Mod. 25.
    V.121-7, Romagosá in GN 15 p. 15.

BM 82	11.34	1	* Romagosa	8.60	3

75. As. O/Pallas, in front P. L. L. L. (without Q). R/Pegasus, with straight wings, wreath above croup, beneath EMPORIT. Mod. 25
    Delgado 276, 277, V.64-4a

MAB 405	9.82	3	Andorra	9.40	12
MAB 412	8.49	-	Baucis	11.70	10
MAB 818	8.49	6	B * Baucis	9.60	10
MAB 966	9.89	3	Baucis	9.10	2
MAB 1026	10.24	5	Baucis	3.65	-
MAB 1120	5.20	-		(halved)	
	(halved)		Pellicer	8.80	9
MAB 1121	10.11	3	Sorjus	9.65	3
M Puig	-	-	Villaronga 1846	12.40	3
A * BM 89	7.67	2	Villaronga 2102	11.20	11
Paris, Luynes 118	7.72	9	Villoldo	5.52	9
Sub ANE 1959 no. 254	15.10	-		(halved)	
Almirall	10.85	3			

76. As. Similar to 75, but pegasus' wings curved towards his head. Mod. 25.
    V.64-4b.

MAB 37	12.78	3	* Almirall	10.30	7
MAB 253	11.32	6	Guadán 4859	10.05	3
MAB 441	8.69	9	Guerin	-	-
MAB 647	5.57	9	Villoldo	13.00	7
MAB 667	11.76	2			

77. Sextans. O/Pallas. R/Pegasus, beneath EM, above P and wreath.
    Mod. 12/14.
    V.123-11, V.64 divisor 1a.

MAB 1020	1.57	10	Ferrer	2.05	1
A * BM 100	1.69	6	B * Grau	-	-
Sub ANE 1965 no. 54	1.20	5	Guadán 340	2.50	6
Almirall	2.40	6	Guadán 4869	1.30	9
Andorra	1.80	11	Villaronga 188	1.84	5
Baucis	2.40	6	Villaronga 604	1.63	10
Baucis	2.00	10	Villoldo	1.88	2
Baucis	1.83	3	Villoldo	1.65	9
Baucis	1.65	-			

78. Sextans. O/Pallas. R/Pegasus, beneath EM. Mod. 12/14.
    V.123-10, V.64 divisor 1b.

A * MAB 217	1.56	2	MAB 922	1.52	6
MAB 228	1.92	3	MAB 1119	0.91	-
MAB 237	1.57	1	B * Almirall	1.55	12

Andorra	1.85	12	Guadán 4873	1.45	6
Andorra	1.80	12	Guerin	-	-
Andorra	1.60	12	Riera	1.70	2
Baucis	1.53	11	Romagosa	1.43	-
Baucis	1.20	7	Villaronga 1863	2.10	10
Guadán 4870	1.60	10	Villaronga 1866	1.90	3

79. Sextans. Similar to no. 78, but inscription IM. Mod. 12/14.

BM 98	2.21	9	Pinta	-	-
BM 101	1.57	11	Sorjus	1.92	9
* Andorra	1.50	7	Sorjus	1.40	4
Barril	-	-	Vall	-	-
Baucis	1.90	4	Villaronga 1864	1.35	12
Guadán 4872	1.60	2			

77/78/79. Indeterminate.

MAB 49	1.82	9	Badía	1.15	-
MAB 1049	1.40	12	Guadán 4871	1.80	3
MAB 1080	1.34	-	Serra	1.95	9
Almirall	1.48	5	Tizón	1.62	12
Almirall	1.41	7	Villaronga 1865	1.60	6
Almirall	1.40	4	Villaronga 2433	1.65	9
Almirall	1.30	6			

80. As. O/Pallas, in front L.C.C.R.Q. R/Pegasus, with wings curved towards his head, wreath above croup, beneath EMPORI or EMPORIT. Mod. 26/27.
V.122-9, V.64-6.

MAB 45	12.64	12	Ferrer	8.80	11
MAB 232	7.52	10	Guadán 4858	7.90	12
MAB 854	10.51	2	* Guerin	-	-
BM 85	13.33	3	Riera	9.55	12
BM 86	12.04	9	Riera	7.75	10
Aldecoa	10.00	2	Tizón	10.00	3
Baucis	7.10	10	Vilaret	10.60	8

SERIES 20

81. As. O/Pallas. R/Pegasus, with curved wings toward his head, wreath above croup, beneath EMPOR, or EMPORI, or EMPORIT. Mod 27.
V.123-5, V.64-7a.

MAB 41	12.61	10	MAB 894	5.82	10
MAB 43	9.01	3	MAB 1085	11.88	6
MAB 231	10.37	11	MAB 1107	9.65	12
MAB 494	12.10	6	MAB 1236	8.52	8
MAB 815	11.89	4	MAB 1286	9.35	4
MAB 858	8.82	8	MAT 3112	7.77	10

M Puig	7.50	–	Riera	11.32	12
M Puig	7.20	–	Riera	9.40	9
IVDJ	–	–	B * Riera	8.00	9
BM 95	6.13	6	Riera	6.85	12
München SNG 112	11.32	12	Romagosa	9.95	3
Sub Circulo X-1962, no. 17	–	–	with countermark dolphin		
			Tizón	8.50	12
Andorra	8.20	9	Tizón	7.15	3
Balsach	10.90	11	Tizón	7.08	4
Baucis	11.62	10	Vilaret	11.10	6
Baucis	10.75	6	with countermark DD and dolphin		
Baucis	9.05	6	Vilaret	10.15	11
Baucis	8.65	3	C * Villaronga 1019	5.65	2
Baucis	8.00	7			
Domenech	8.20	6	Villaronga 1849	12.65	6
Ferrer	11.00	12			
Ferrer	10.80	2			
A * Guadán 325	11.00	2			
Guadán 3120	4.50	12			
Guadán 4861	11.20	9			
Pellicer	12.00	12			
Pellicer	7.50	3			

82. As. Similar to 81, but reverse inscription EMPOR, MP in ligature. (Some reverses are the same die as no. 83.) Mod. 27. V.64-7b.

BM 96	10.49	4	* Andorra	9.85	7
Sub ANE 1965 no. 52	13.60	3	Baucis	8.75	4
Almirall	6.55	3			

81-82. Indeterminate, all halved.

MAB	4.91	3	Nuix	3.85	–
Almirall	6.45	–	Tizón	5.10	–
Espuny	3.80	–			

SERIES 21

83. As. O/Pallas, in front P.I.P.C.S.M.Q. R/Pegasus, with curved wings toward his head, wreath above croup, beneath EMPOR, MP in ligature. (Some reverses are the same die as no. 82.) Mod. 27 V.122-8, V.64-8a.

* MAB 224	9.39	3	Riera	10.95	7
Almirall	10.95	2	Villoldo	10.24	5
Almirall	7.25	7			

84. As. Similar to 83, but reverse inscription EMPOR or EMPORI, without ligature. Mod. 27.
H. III-6, V.64-8b.

MAB 302	6.11	1	Baucis	10.30	12
	(halved)		Cruxent	12.50	12
MAB 345	3.48	9	Guadán 319	10.00	6
	(halved)		Riera	12.60	6
A * Andorra	7.60	5	Riera	9.70	2
Andorra	3.00	12	Riera	9.15	2
	(halved)		B* Tizón	12.50	12
Almirall	7.21	3	Vilaret	9.15	6

85. As. O/Pallas, in front C.I.NICOM, behind P.FL, beneath Q.
R/Pegasus, with curved wings toward his head, wreath above croup, beneath EMPORI or EMPORIT. Mod. 27/28.
V. 121-10, H.III-4, V.64-9.

A * BM 87	13.05	9	Baucis	5.33	12
Almirall	10.52	9		(halved)	
Andorra	9.70	7	B * Romagosa	11.70	12
Andorra	5.26	6	Sorjus	10.18	3
	(halved)		Tizón	9.46	7
Baucis	8.80	11	Vilaret	10.60	4
			Vilaronga 1062	10.30	5

86. As. O/Pallas, in front C.I.NICOM, behind P.FL, beneath Q.
R/Pegasus, with curved wings toward his head, wreath above croup, beneath EMPORI, in exergue P.FL, before pegasus Q. Mod. 27.
V.121-9, V.64-9 bis.

BM 88	10.50	10	*Tizón	10.95	6
Paris, 117	-	-	Villaronga	8.15	2
Guadán 314	8.00	2			

87. Sextans. O/Pallas. R/Pegasus, with curved wings toward his head, wreath above croup, beneath EMP. Mod. 14.
V.123-9, V.64 div. 2.

MAB 50	2.65	12	Andorra	1.70	9
MAB 294	1.38	10	Andorra	1.50	7
MAB 695	2.07	-	Baucis	2.20	2
MAB 1259	2.94	6	* Baucis	1.40	7
MAB 1566	1.71	9	Vilaret	1.50	3
BM 99	1.80	5	Vilaret	1.40	3
Sub ANE 1965 no. 55	1.20	9	Villaronga 2103	1.60	3
Andorra	2.78	5	Villoldo	1.48	5

88. As. O/Pallas, in front C.P.C.M.S.R.Q. R/Pegasus, with curved wings toward his head, wreath above, beneath EMPOR or EMPORI. Mod. 26.
V.122-7, V.64-10.

A * MAB 47	9.79	11	Guerin	-	-
MAB 855	7.19	8	Guerin	-	-
MAB 1128	10.15	9	Pellicer	11.70	6
MAB 1397	3.43	-	Riera	11.40	10
	(halved)		Riera	11.27	6
MAT 2557	7.83	3	Sorjus	11.16	6
M Puig	9.80	-	Tizón	12.35	7
B * BM 91	7.39	11	Villaret	8.65	5
BM 92	10.74	3	Villaronga 258	9.95	9
Andorra	9.40	7	Villaronga 646	10.70	4
Guadan 318	8.90	12	Villoldo	8.00	10

SERIES 22

89. As. O/Pallas, in front L.M.RVF.P.C.Q. (RVF in ligature). R/Pegasus, with curved wings toward his head, wreath above croup, beneath EMPOR or EMPORIT. Mod. 26/27.
V.122-10, V.64-11.

MAB 387	5.15	2	Guadán 322	10.30	2
	(halved)		Guadán 4856	9.65	4
MAB 1392	5.48	-	Guadán 4857	10.90	9
	(halved)		Pinta	-	-
M Puig	9.52	-	Riera	13.20	7
M Puig	7.60	-	Riera	11.60	6
A * BM 107	10.52	7	Riera	-	-
BM 108	12.74	2	Serra	9.30	2
BM 109	8.08	7	Sorjus	9.81	12
Paris, Luynes	11.91	5	B * Tizón	9.70	12
München SNG 110	8.42	10	Vall	-	-
Almirall	12.31	4	Villaret	11.90	7
Almirall	9.14	11	Villaronga 688	12.18	11
Andorra	13.90	7	Villaronga 864	8.00	7
Baucis	11.85	1	Villaronga 1572	9.50	7
Baucis	10.75	11	Villaronga 1850	12.40	8
Baucis	8.70	10	Villoldo	11.10	2
Cullell	8.70	7	Villoldo	7.04	2
Guadán 320	11.30	2		(halved)	
Guadan 321	9.80	12	Col part.	-	2

SERIES 23

90. As. O/Pallas, in front M.O.L.A.Q. R/Pegasus, with curved wings toward his head, wreath above croup, beneath EMPOR. Mod. 28.
V.122-6, V.64-12a.

MAB 38	9.60	9	Grau	-	11
BM 111	12.12	6	Rectoret	-	-
Baucis	12.06	6	*Villaret	12.80	6

91. As. O/Pallas, in front M.O.H.L.A.F.Q. R/Pegasus, with curved wings toward his head, wreath above croup, beneath EMPOR. Mod. 28.
V.123-1, V.12b.

MAB 913	9.15	2	Baucis	3.35	12
MAB 1574	6.00	6		(halved)	
	(halved)		* Riera	11.90	3
Aldecoa	9.10	12	Villaret	10.60	9
Barril	-	-	Villoldo	11.10	7

92. As. Similar to 91, but unusual wings.
V.64-12c.

* Almirall	11.43	7

93. As. O/Pallas, in front P.C.PV.Q.C.C.Q, P and V in ligature. R/Pegasus, unusual wings, wreath above croup, beneath EMPOR. Mod. 27/28.
V.123-2, V.64-13.

MAB 44	14.41	11	Balsach	11.35	10
MAB 259	4.55	2	Balsach	7.65	11
	(halved)		Cardim	7.00	12
MAB 436	9.70	2	Baucis	4.35	12
MAT 1971	7.54	5		(halved)	
MAT 2558	8.49	5	Guadán 323	10.50	2
BM 112	13.52	2	Guadán 324	10.20	3
BM 113	8.77	9	* Guerin	-	-
München SNG 111	12.08	3	Riera	9.15	3
Aldecoa	12.20	10	Sorjus	12.76	4
Almirall	11.74	2	Villaronga 863	12.10	4
Almirall	9.90	6	Villoldo	10.15	3

SERIES 24

94. As. O/Pallas, in front C.S.B.L.C.M.Q. R/Pegasus, with curved wings toward his head, wreath above croup, beneath EMPORIT. Mod. 27.
V.122-1, V.64-14.

MAB 261	10.52	11	Baucis	8.70	12
MAB 921	4.98	2	Baucis	3.30	2
	(halved)			(halved)	
*BM 105	10.52	6	Vidal	11.00	4
			Villaronga 1853	10.75	6

95. As. O/Pallas, in front CN.C.P.C.M.A., beneath Q. R/Pegasus, unusual wings, wreath above croup, beneath EMPORIT. Mod 27/28.
   V.123-4, V.64-15a.

MAB 226	4.03	9	* Cardim	9.00	2
	(halved)		Romagosa	12.40	11
MAB 650	4.72	6	Villaronga 1341	14.35	3
	(halved)		Villaronga 1695	9.55	11
MAB 830	10.67	8	Villaronga 1851	5.70	12
MAB 1443	5.26	-		(halved)	
	(halved)		Villaronga 1852	11.95	3
BM 104	12.03	2			
Almirall	9.82	7			
Baucis	12.70	4			
Baucis	9.07	6			

96. As. Similar to 95, but inscription CN beneath head and C.P.C.M.A.Q. in front. Mod. 27.
   V.123-3, V.64-15b.

* Almirall	10.47	12

97. As. O/Pallas, in front CN.C.GR.L.C.F., beneath Q. R/Pegasus, wreath of dots above croup, beneath EMPORI or EMPORIT. Mod. 27/28.
   V.122-2 with EMPORIT and V.122-4 with EMPORI, V.64-16.

MAB 1241	3.71	-	Riera	12.00	12
	(halved)		* Tizón	12.74	6
BM 123	10.65	2	Villoldo	11.15	9
Paris, Luynes 97	9.55	5	Villoldo	9.72	6
Milano	-	-	Villoldo	3.72	12
Andorra	12.25	12		(halved)	
Cruxent	-	-			
	(halved)				

98. As. Similar to 97, but inscription with A at end. Mod. 27.
   Romagosa, Gaceta Numismatica 15, 16.

* M Puig	-	-	Almirall	6.65	3
Sub Krass VI-64 no. 468	-	-	Ferrer	7.00	7

99. As. O/Pallas, in front C.CA.T.C.O.CA, beneath Q. R/Pegasus, wreath of dots above croup, beneath EMPOR or EMPORI. Mod. 27/28.
   H.III-5.

MAB 230	6.98	12	Cullell	9.50	3
MAB 918	10.16	6	Grau	-	-
IVDJ	-	-	Guadán 315	11.00	3
BM 119	9.77	5	Guadán 316	10.50	12
* BM 120	8.50	6	Rectoret	-	-
BM 122	9.78	6	Riera	11.56	9
Paris, Luynes 95	7.56	11	Riera	10.70	12
Almirall	8.22	5	Sanz	-	5
Andorra	9.90	12	Tizón	14.55	6
Baucis	9.50	6	Tizón	7.70	12
Cardim	9.70	6			

100. As. Similar to 99, but inscription with R at end, sometimes CAR in ligature. Mod. 27/28.
V.122-3, V.64-17.

MAB 631	11.26	12	SNG München 107	12.62	12
MAB 857	9.92	3	Almirall	12.54	3
BM 115	12.82	3	Tizón	10.00	5
A * BM 116	10.86	2	Vilaret	11.15	6
B * BM 117	9.61	5	Villaronga 1338	9.20	3
BM 121	7.21	6	Villaronga 1701	9.92	12
Milano	-	-	Villoldo	8.42	3

99-100 - Indeterminate.

MAB 1082	1.78 (halved)	-	MAB 1290	12.18	12
			BM 118	7.42	12
MAB 882	6.36 (halved)	12	Sub ANE 1965 no. 51	9.05	12
MAB 914	6.71 (halved)	12	Andorra	5.50 (halved)	12
MAB 1287	8.68	6	Baucis	8.50	6
			Tizón	11.00	6

101. As. O/Pallas, in front C.T.C.Q.C.C., beneath Q. R/Pegasus, wreath above croup, beneath EMPOR. Mod. 26.
V.121-4.

GNC	-	-
* BM 106	10.10	1
Ruscino	11.80	-

102. As. O/Pallas, in front C.O.C.C.M.A., beneath Q. R/Pegasus, wreath above croup, beneath EMPOR. Mod. 27.
V.122-5, V.64-18.

MAB 528	5.03 (halved)	6	A * Paris, Luynes 104	10.87	7
MAB 1071	4.51 (halved)	-	SNG München 108	10.32	7
BM 114	14.31	2	Almirall	6.40	3

Barril	-	-	Riera	9.20	1
B * Guadán 317	10.00	6	Romagosa	6.30	2
Guadán 4835	10.75	3			

103. As. Similar to 103, but Q in front.

Baucis	12.75	6	*Villaronga 3780	9.40	3
Tizón	8.06	6	Villoldo	12.32	11

104. As. O/Pallas, in front M.A.B.M.F., beneath (M) Q. R/Pegasus, wreath of dots above croup, beneath EMPOR. Mod. 26/27. V.121-6.

* BM 103	7.58	7

105. As. Similar to 104, but MQ behind Pallas, and wreath with dots joined.

A * MAB 46	10.82	3	SNG München 109	7.12	6
MAB 1191	-	11	B*Romagosa	12.13	-
Paris, Luynes 107	10.82	6	Tizón	11.00	3

106. As. O/Pallas, in front M.A.B.M.F.M., behind Q. R/Pegasus, linear wreath above croup, beneath EMPOR. Mod. 27. V.121-5, V.63-19.

MAB 313	5.27 (halved)	8	Cardim	11.00	3
			Guadán 313	10.00	9
BM 102	12.02	2	Guadán 4860	9.50	1
*Paris, Luynes 119	11.86	5	Villaronga 5321	13.32	-
Baucis	10.85	5			

SERIES 25

107. As. O/Pallas with small head. R/Pegasus, wreath of dots above croup, beneath EMPOR Mod. 27/28. V.123-7, V.64-20.

MAB 39	16.12	6	MAB 1488	-	12
MAB 48	9.04	12	MAT 1958	7.35	3
MAB 611	5.08 (halved)	8	MAT 2559	13.07	3
			MAT 3248	9.24	12
MAB 763	9.22	3	BM 124	13.02	7
MAB 880	15.73	9	A * BM 130	8.51	9
MAB 885	5.94 (halved)	2	BM 131	8.41	4
			Almirall	10.80	9
MAB 888	5.65 (halved)	12	Almirall	8.95	6
			Andorra	9.80	9
MAB 895	7.10	3	Balsach	7.00	2
MAB 1009	12.73	1	Baucis	8.38	2
MAB 1242	5.95 (halved)	-	Baucis	7.40	9
			Cardim	9.90	12
MAB 1289	5.11 (halved)	-	Cullell	8.45	12
			Ferrer	6.40	12

Grau	-	2	Vilaret	13.90	12
Guadán 2047	12.20	6	Vilaret	8.55	2
B * Guadán 4863	15.00	6	Villaronga 139	9.27	12
Guerin	-	-	Villaronga 303	8.40	12
Riera	13.65	9	Villaronga 862	9.36	9
Riera	9.80	12	Villaronga 1854	10.15	11
Riera	8.60	4	Villaronga 1855	9.40	5
Riera	7.80	12	Villoldo	9.38	12
Tizón	12.00	3	Col part.	-	2
Tizón	8.90	6	Col part.	-	-
Tizón	8.80	11			

108. Quadrans. O/Pallas, R/Pegasus, beneath EM. Mod. 16/17.
V.123-12, V.64, divisor 3.

MAB 236	2.94	3	Baucis	2.55	9
MAB 344	2.56	12	Ferrer	2.80	12
MAB 806	2.35	6	Ferrer	2.20	5
MAB 821	-	3	Guerin	-	-
MAB 917	2.39	6	Guerin	-	-
Almirall	2.90	3	Nuix	2.18	12
Almirall	2.30	12	Sorjus	2.38	12
Andorra	2.62	12	Vidal	2.80	6
Andorra	2.32	4	Villaronga 142	2.47	5
Andorra	2.30	11	Villaronga 1862	3.20	9
* Baucis	2.60	9	Villoldo	2.65	12

109. AS. O/Pallas with large head. R/Pegasus, wreath of dots above croup, beneath EMPOR. Mod. 27/28.
V.123-6, V.64-21.

MAB 367	5.15 (halved)	6	Sub ANE 1963 no. 105	8.20	-
MAB 867	6.37 (halved)	12	Almirall	9.90	5
			Amirall	8.40	12
MAB 1002	4.98 (halved)	12	Andorra	14.70	6
			Andorra	13.70	6
MAB 1060	4.57 (halved)	-	Barril	-	-
			Baucis	11.15	6
MAB 1305	4.24 (halved)	-	Baucis	9.50	11
			Baucis	7.50	11
MAB 1391	5.04 (halved)	-	Baucis	5.20 (halved)	12
M Puig	8.48	-	Grau	-	-
BM 125	12.31	6		(halved)	
BM 126	12.15	7	Guadán 327	10.90	12
BM 127	10.70	6	Guadán 329	10.10	12
BM 128	14.74	5	Guadán 4862	8.50	5
BM 129	10.44	6	A * Guerin	-	-
SNG München 113	11.64	3	Lizana	9.00	-

Nuix	9.05	12	Sorjus	11.79	6
Riera	12.82	12	Tizón	14.00	6
Riera	10.40	2	Tizón	10.80	6
B * Riera	10.15	6	Villoldo	16.10	6
Riera	8.30	6	Villoldo	10.00	6
Riera	7.50 (halved)	12			

SERIES 26

110. As. Countermark dolphin above helmet and countermark D.D. in front of Pallas, on the issue no. 107. Mod. 27/28. V.123-8.

MAB 849	–	12	Baucis	3.30	12
MAB 853	–	7		(halved)	
MAB 871	–	–	B * Cardim	12.42	1
MAB 998	–	6	Cardim	10.20	12
MAB 1057	–	11	Cardim	9.30	7
MAB 1058	6.47 (halved)	6	Ferrer	14.10	2
			Ferrer	10.00	3
MAB 1072	8.02	–	Ferrer	8.90	1
MAT 2639	9.22	1	Guadán	12.10	3
MAT 2656	8.00	9	Guerin	–	–
BM 136	4.62	1	Guerin	–	–
Paris, Luynes 87	8.91	9	Guerin	–	–
Condé-sur-Aisne 329	10.82	–	Guerin	–	–
Condé-sur-Aisne 328	10.37	–	Pagés	–	–
Sub ANE 1965 no. 53	7.10	–	Rectoret	–	–
Sub ANE VI-1970 no. 34	–	–	Riera	15.30	6
			Riera	13.60	12
Sub Circulo III-1975 no. 71	71.00	–	Riera	8.70	12
			Sanz	–	6
Aldecoa	7.90	12	Sorjus	8.59	6
Almirall	11.00	6	Tizón	9.05	9
Almirall	8.80	4	Tizón	8.50	3
Almirall	11.38	3	Víctor Catalá	10.02	9
Andorra	10.40	6	Vilaret	13.50	8
Badia	10.65	–	Vilaret	9.00	7
A * Baucis	12.70	9	Villaronga 1856	9.60	7
Baucis	11.80	5	Vilaronga 1858	9.30	6
Baucis	11.75	5	Villaronga 1859	10.50	3
Baucis	9.10	4	Col part.	–	11
Baucis	8.30	2	Col part.	–	12
Baucis	4.90 (halved)	12			

111. As. Countermark dolphin above helmet and countermark D.D. in front of Pallas, on the issue no. 109. Mod. 27/28.

MAB 35	5.27	-	MAB 1004	-	12
	(halved)		MAB 1005	-	12
MAB 242	9.09	6	MAB 1006	-	6
MAB 249	12.89	6	MAB 1012	-	-
MAB 252	11.78	12	MAB 1013	-	3
MAB 255	6.22	6	MAB 1015	-	6
	(halved)		MAB 1025	7.13	2
MAB 270	5.76	12		(halved)	
	(halved)		MAB 1036	-	6
MAB 279	9.14	6	MAB 1050	5.91	6
MAB 281	13.38	4		(halved)	
MAB 295	10.87	6	MAB 1059	8.46	-
MAB 304	10.97	6		(halved)	
MAB 305	12.26	12	MAB 1067	7.70	6
MAB 312	3.29	12	MAB 1091	8.16	6
	(halved)		MAB 1097	7.99	6
MAB 338	6.75	6	MAB 1098	8.97	7
MAB 381	3.92	-	MAB 1130	13.42	12
	(halved)		MAB 1139	8.33	6
MAB 479	5.97	-	MAB 1147	10.81	6
MAB 579	5.27	-	MAB 1176	-	3
	(halved)		MAB 1228	4.20	6
MAB 614	10.23	4		(halved)	
MAB 624	11.15	11	MAB 1237	10.33	6
MAB 642	7.10	6	MAB 1282	19.08	6
MAB 659	7.63	12	MAB 1297	8.37	-
MAB 664	8.01	6	MAB 1317	-	-
MAB 689	4.70	-	MAB 1377	4.08	-
	(halved)			(halved)	
MAB 696	2.34	-	MAB 1379	3.39	-
	(halved)			(halved)	
MAB 699	2.99	-	MAB 1393	5.65	-
	(halved)			(halved)	
MAB 831	-	12	MAB 1395	3.27	-
MAB 846	-	6		(halved)	
MAB 876	-	12	MAB 1448	-	-
MAB 879	-	6	MAB 1481	-	6
MAB 883	5.14	2	MAB 1494	-	-
	(halved)		MAB 1504	-	2
MAB 884	-	9	MAT 1970	11.89	6
MAB 887	9.38	11	MAT 2556	12.02	6
	(halved)		Porqueres (Banyoles)	-	-
MAB 915	13.25	12	BM 132	10.01	12
MAB 916	10.48	6	BM 133	8.32	6
MAB 976	5.12	-	BM 134	8.32	6
	(halved)		BM 135	9.24	12
MAB 996	6.33	6	Sub Circulo III-	-	-
	(halved)		1966 no. 75		

Almirall	15.00	12	Guadán 4868	7.40	–
Almirall	14.35	3		(halved)	
Almirall	14.15	6	Guerin	–	–
Almirall	12.70	11	Nuix	8.00	5
Almirall	11.74	6	Pagés	–	7
Almirall	10.92	5	Pellicer	9.25	6
Almirall	10.40	3	Rectoret	–	–
Almirall	9.80	5	Riera	15.18	6
Almirall	9.60	4	Riera	14.20	11
Almirall	9.40	5	Riera	13.50	12
Almirall	4.69	–	Riera	11.40	6
	(halved)		Riera	9.60	5
Almirall	4.30	7	Riera	6.05	11
Andorra	7.85	6	Romagosa	3.80	–
Andorra	5.40	12		(halved)	
Andorra	–	12	Serra	6.55	7
Balsach	8.95	7	Sorjus	10.83	3
Barril	–	–	Sorjus	–	2
Baucis	12.15	6	Tizón	10.45	6
Baucis	11.20	12	B * Tizón	9.00	8
Baucis	10.45	6	Tizón	7.20	11
A * Baucis	9.20	6	Vall	–	–
Baucis	9.00	1	Vall	–	–
Baucis	8.62	2	Vidal	9.20	12
Baucis	7.90	12	Vilaret	12.10	12
Baucis	5.60	12	Vilaret	10.10	6
	(halved)		Vilaret	9.20	12
Baucis	5.45	12	Villaronga 140	9.80	1
	(halved)		Villaronga 141	12.10	12
Baucis	5.20	12	Villaronga 861	11.15	12
	(halved)		Villaronga 1857	9.50	12
Cardim	10.60	6	Villaronga 1860	7.25	–
Cullell	9.20	3		(halved)	
Cullell	9.00	6	Villoldo	13.35	11
Cullell	6.70	12	Villoldo	11.10	11
Ferrer	9.80	12	Villoldo	8.72	6
Ferrer	9.60	6	Villoldo	6.90	12
Guadán 331	8.50	6		(halved)	
Guadán 335	11.00	12	Col part.	–	6
Guadán 336	11.50	4	Col part.	12.70	6
Guadán 1872	10.50	12			
Guadán 4865	11.40	1			
Guadán 4866	11.20	6			
Guadán 4867	6.60	–			
	(halved)				

112. As. Irregular position of countermark DD and dolphin on coins no. 107 and 109.

    A) Dolphin only on obverse.

* Almirall	11.41	6

B) DD only on obverse. V.64 no. 14, 15.

Paris, Luynes 86	10.11	9	Villoldo	12.86	6
Baucis	11.62	10	* Villoldo	10.10	1
Guadán 330	10.00	6			

C) DD only on reverse. V.64 no. 11.

Milano	-	-	Riera	8.70	11
Aldecoa	10.20	12	* Villaronga 3878	11.10	12
Baucis	12.10	11			

D) Countermark DD on obverse and reverse. V.64 no. 12, 13.

* Baucis	11.02	12	Villaronga 1063	8.55	7
Villaronga 275	14.60	6			

E) Countermark dolphin and DD on obverse and DD on reverse. V.64 no. 10.

Baucis	9.32	6	Riera	7.90	12
* Nuix	12.75	4			

F) Countermark dolphin and DD on obverse and dolphin on reverse. V.64 no. 8.

* Villaronga 1861	11.15	6

SERIES 27

113. As. Countermark two palms on obverse on coin without names of magistrates.
Guadán LXXXVIII, V.64 no. 17.

Berlin - -

114. As. Countermark eagle's head on obverse on coin with indeterminate names of magistrates.

* Balsach 12.25 5

115. As. Countermark sword and DD on obverse and D on reverse.

* Paris 92 10.65 12

116. As. Countermark herring-bone.
On obverse V. 64 no. 18.

A * Nuix 8.10 11

On reverse Guadán LXXXII, V.64 no. 19.

The Hague, Hill III-2	9.49	-
B * BM 90	11.16	6

117. As. Countermark N.
   On obverse with dolphin and DD.
   Guadán LXXXV, Delgado 292, V.64 no. 9.
   On obverse with dolphin.
   Guadán LXXXIII-LXXXIV, V.64 no. 16.
   On reverse, N alone.

* Pagés   -   6

118. As. Countermark N10 alone on reverse.
   Guadán LXXXIX, V.64 no. 6.

Berlin   -   -

119. As. Countermark IMI. BT on obverse.
   Guadán LXXIX, V.64 no. 5.

* Almirall   7.81   7

120. As. Countermark NUMEL on obverse.
   Guadán LXXXVII, V.64 no. 4.

MAN   -   -

121. As. Countermark PMP on obverse.
   Guadán LXXXVI, V.64 no. 3.

Delgado 293   -   -

SERIES 28

122. As. O/Rectangular board with VL in ligature, fasces on the sides.
   R/Possible altar, with three crossed parallel lines coming from
   opposite corners, perhaps a letter R right, and with a vertical
   line from the top of the altar. Mod. 12.

   J. M. NUIX y L. VILLARONGA, <u>Sobre unas raras monedas
   emporitanas,</u> Miscelánea Arqueológica, II, Barcelona 1974, 81-86.

A * Guadán 3105	2.20	6	B * MAB 51	1.67	8
Víctor Catalá 410	3.26	-	MAB 532	2.63	4
Víctor Catalá 411	3.10	-	MAB 575	2.81	6
Víctor Catalá 412	2.76	-	MAB 597	2.84	8
Víctor Catalá 413	2.67	-	C * MAB 598	3.11	-
Victor Catalá 414	2.59	-	MAB 626	3.41	3
Víctor Catalá 415	2.54	-	MAB 739	2.03	-
Víctor Catalá 416	2.20	-	MAB 750	2.39	-
Víctor Catalá 417	2.16	-	MAB 808	2.09	-
Víctor Catalá 418	2.03	-	MAB 1136	3.25	9

NOTES

1. For all references to Emporion in the ancient texts, see M. Almagro, Las fuentes escritas referentes a Ampurias, Barcelona 1951.

2. Appian, Iber 7.

3. Polybius, Historia I, 3, 76.

4. T. Livy, Historia XXXIV, 8.

5. T. Livy, Historia XXXIV, 9.

6. T. Livy, Historia XXXIV, 11 and 13.

7. Sallust, Historia 5.

8. Pliny, Historia Naturalis III, 21-22.

9. Strabo, Geografia III, 4, 8.

10. Stephen of Byzantium, Ethnica.

11. A. Furtwangler, Le trésor d'Auriol, printing; Remarques sur les plus anciennes monnaies Frappées en Espagne, Schweizar Münzblätter 21, 1971, 13-21.

12. J. Amoros, D'una trobella de monedes emporitanes i la cronologia de les monedes d'Empuries, Barcelona 1933; Les monedes emporitanes anteriors a les dracmes, Barcelona 1934.

13. J. Amoros, Les dracmes emporitanes, Barcelona 1933. A. M. de Guadan, Las monedas de plata de Emporion y Rhode, Barcelona 1968-70. The chronology proposed by Guadan is based on the date given by Sydenham for the introduction of the Roman denarius, that is 187 B.C.; however, the revision of this date and the general acceptance of 211 B.C. alters the chronology of the coins of Emporion, the general lines of which we have set out. See note 2 of p. 92 of J. C. M. Richard and L. Villaronga, Recherches sur les étalons monétaires en Espagne et en Gaule du sud, antérieurement à l'epoque d'Auguste, Melanges de la Casa de Velazquez, IX, 1973.

14. L. Villaronga, Las monedas hispano-cartaginesas, Barcelona 1973.

15. M. Campo, Los divisores de la dracma emporitana, Acta Numismática II, 1972, 19-48.

16. M. Crawford, The Financial organization of republican Spain, Numismatic Chronicle 1969, 79-93.

17. C. Pujol y Camps, Empuries. Catálogo de sus monedas e imitaciones Memorial Numismatico Español III, 1873, 3-46, 65-95, 121-189.

18. A. Delgado, <u>Nuevo método de clasificación de las medallas autónomas de España</u>, vol. III, Sevilla 1876. The section on the coins of Emporion, by C. Pujol y Camps, pages 114 to 234 and plates CXXIV to CXLII.

19. J. Zobel de Zangroniz, <u>Estudio Histórico de la moneda antiqua de España,</u> Memorial Numismático Español IV, V, 1878-80, especially pp. 28-29 of vol. V.

20. A. Vives Escudero, <u>La moneda Hispánica,</u> Madrid 1926.

21. C. F. Hill, <u>Notes on the ancient coinage of Hispania Citerior,</u> New York 1931.

22. A. Beltran, <u>Curso de Numismática,</u> vol. I, Cartagena 1950. <u>Sobre algunas monedas bilingües romanas del municipio de Ampurias,</u> Numisma 3, 1952.

23. M. Grant, <u>From Imperium to auctoritas,</u> Cambridge, 1946.

24. A. M. de Guadan, <u>Numismática ibérica e ibero-romana,</u> Madrid 1969.

25. J. Untermann, <u>Monumenta Linguarum Hispanicarum,</u> Weisbaden 1975.

26. L. Villaronga, <u>Sistematización del bronce ibérico emporitano,</u> Acta Numismática II, 1972, 49-86.

27. L. Villaronga, <u>Los magistrados en las amonedaciones latinas de Emporiae,</u> en Estudios de Numismática Romana, Barcelona 1964.

28. Pere Vegué, director of the Gabinete Numismático de Catalunya, has brought to the author's attention coin no. 33, 622, with the symbol of Victory without the prow, and semis no. 33, 636. Roger Grau de Elne pointed out the coin with a Greek letter phi above the Pegasus, another example of which was later found by the author. Untermann's work has brought to the author's knowledge two coins from the Gabinete Numismático de Catalunya; no. 30159 with a lion and the inscription ETABAN and no. 3342 with a lion and EBOR. To the Latin series is added the issue with magistrates names C.T.C.Q.C.CA., represented by a coin in the British Museum which was brought to the author's notice by O - C. M. Richard and T. Hillgarth. Some variants of inscriptions in other issues have also been added.

29. Pliny, <u>Historia Natural</u> 3, 21.

30. F. Mateu y Llopis, <u>Topónimos monetales en el dominio catalan,</u> Boletín de Dialectologia Catalana XXXIV, 1956-57, 782-795.

31. M. Almagro, <u>Las fuentes escritas referentes a Ampurias,</u> Barcelona 1951; <u>Ampurias, historia de la ciudad y quia de las excavaciones,</u> Barcelona 1951.

32. E. Sanmarti, <u>Acerca del periodo tardorrepublicano en Empuries,</u> Acta Numismático III, 1973, 11-24.

33. M. Grant, <u>From Imperium to auctoritas,</u> Cambridge, reprinted 1969, p. 154ff.

34. <u>SNG Lockett III,</u> no. 1021-23.

35. SNG Deutschland, München II, no. 139-143.
36. SNG American Numismatic Society I, no. 699ff.
37. SNG American Numismatic Society I, no. 526ff.
38. Crawf. 41/7b.
39. LMPER I, 264-266.
40. H. de la Tour, Atles des monnaies gauloises, Paris 1892 plates III and IV.
41. RIC I, 58.
42. RIC no. 329 and addition.
43. LMPER, 273 and ff.
44. Muret Chabouillet, Catalogue des monnaies gauloises de la Bibliothèque Nationale, Paris 1889, no. 1475 and ff.
45. Giesecke, Sicilia Numismatica, Leipzig 1923, plates, 19, no. 7 and 8.
46. Saussaye, Numismatique de la Narbonnaise, Paris 1842.
47. SNG Lockett, no. 999.
48. SNG Danish Museum, North Africa-Carthage, no. 94-98.
49. Crawf. plate I.
50. R. Thomsen, Early Roman Coinage, I, figs. 16, 17, 18 and 19.
51. Giesecke, Sicilia Numismatica, Leipzig 1923, plate 15 no. 11.
52. SNG American Numismatic Society I, no. 17-18.
53. SNG Deutschland, München II, nos. 154-157, 417-419, 429-430.
54. Crawf. 39/3.
55. SNG American Numismatic Society I, nos. 635-639.
56. V. 68-10, 69-7 and 9.
57. J. M. Nuix and L. Villaronga, Sobre unas raras monedas emporitanas, Miscelánea Arqueológica, II, Barcelona 1974, pp. 81-86.
58. LMPER nos. 724-734.
59. V. plate 74.
60. V. plates 68 to 70.
61. Crawf. 39/4.
62. V. 24-7 and 12; 31-10; 32-6 and 12; 33-3 and 14.
63. V. plate 19.
64. Crawf. 157/1.
65. V. 34-4.
66. Crawf. 116.

67. <u>Crawf.</u> 142/1.

68. <u>V.</u> plate 23.

69. <u>Crawf.</u> 22/1.

70. <u>Crawf.</u> 235/1.

71. <u>V.</u> 32-14.

72. <u>V.</u> 23-4.

73. <u>Crawf.</u> 296/1.

74. <u>Crawf.</u> 312/2.

75. <u>V.</u> 21-5.

76. <u>V.</u> plate 26.

77. <u>V.</u> 34-8, 9 and 10.

78. <u>V.</u> 22-12.

79. <u>V.</u> 29-3 and 4.

80. <u>Crawf.</u> 61/1.

81. <u>Crawf.</u> 61/2 to 8 and 144.

82. <u>LMPER</u> no. 749.

83. L. Villaronga, <u>La evolución epigráfica en las leyendas monetales ibéricas</u>, Numisma 30, 1958, 9-50.

84. L. Villaronga, <u>Las marcas de valor en las monedas de Undicescen,</u> VIII Congreso Nacional de Arquelogia de Sevilla, 1963, 331-338.

85. For this mark and the following see: L. Villaronga, <u>Las marcas de valor en monedas ibéricas,</u> VII Congreso Nacional de Arquelogia de Jaén, 1971, 531-537.

86. <u>MLH, 168,</u> d - 10 with some hesitation interprets this sign as the Iberian TAN. The author has never found this possibility amongst the many coins he has examined.

87. Tovar, <u>ELH,</u> page 17, states conclusively that Basque is not Iberian, but accepts that some ancient relationship exists between Celtic and Basque and that there are similarities between Basque and Iberian, which, though limited, are indisputable, and include certain interdependancies. This method was first used by D. Pio Beltran, and is the one followed by the author.

88. <u>MLH</u> p. 165.

89. Frevier, <u>Histoire de l'Ecriture,</u> Paris 1959, p. 584.

90. <u>MLH</u> p. 171.

91. Tovar see note 87.

92. <u>MLH</u>, p. 168, reads inscription 5 as SESTEN, after M. Gomez Moreno, <u>miscelaneas,</u> p. 315, with a last letter which we have not found on the coins we have studied. <u>MLH,</u> p. 171, thinks that this reading is doubtful.

93. A. Villoldo, <u>Algunas monedas ibéricas poco conocidas,</u> Numisma 69, 1964, p. 23. A. M. Guadan, <u>Tipologia de las contramarcas en la amonedacion ibero-romana,</u> Numario Hispanico 17, 1960, 104, CXLVII.

94. <u>MLH</u> p. 171.

95. <u>MLH</u> pp. 170-171.

96. Tovar, <u>Estudios de las primitives lenguas hispanas,</u> p. 154 and ff.

97. M. Gomez Moreno, <u>Miscelaneas,</u> Madrid 1949, p. 233.

98. L. Villaronga, <u>Las monedas de Arse-Saguntum,</u> Barcelona 1967, p. 77.

99. <u>CIL</u> 3621, 2740, 6144, and <u>MLI</u> XV.

100. J. Untermann, <u>Elementos de un atlas antroponímico de la Hispania Antigua,</u> Madrid 1965.

101. <u>ELH</u> 370-372.

102. <u>ELH</u> 371 and 382.

103. <u>ELH</u> 371 and 382.

104. <u>MLH</u> 169-170.

105. <u>V. 64</u> 83.

106. <u>CIL</u> II, 165.

107. <u>MLH</u> 160.

108. Inscription 1 of M. Almagro, <u>Las inscriptiones ampuritanas, griegas, ibéricas y latinas,</u> Barcelona 1952.

109. Inscription no. 3 of M. Almagro, cited in the previous note.

110. A. Heiss, <u>Description Générale des Monnaies antiques de l'Espagne,</u> Paris 1870, 75.

111. <u>CIL</u> 3840.

112. M. Almagro, <u>Las necrópolis de Ampurias,</u> II. Barcelona 1955, 25.

113. <u>CIL</u> II, 985, 2029, 1460. M. Grant, <u>From imperium to auctoritas,</u> Cambridge 1969, 156-157.

114. <u>RIC</u> 74-75.

115. A. M. de Guadan, <u>Tipologia de las contramarcas en la amoneda-ibero-romana,</u> Numario Hispánico 17, 1960, 7-22. E. Ripoll, D. M. Nuix and L. Villaronga, <u>La contramarca Delfín y DD en las monedas emporitanas,</u> paper given at the III Congreso Nacional de Numismatica.

Summary in E. Ripoll, J. M. Nuix and L. Villaronga, <u>Consecuencias del estudio estadístico de las monedas halladas en las excavaciones de Emporion,</u> paper given at the Methoden Kolloqium of the FMRD, Frankfurt Feb. 1976.

116. J. C. M. Richard and L. Villaronga, <u>Recherches sur les étalons monétaires en Espagne et en Gaule du sud, antérieurement à l'époque d'Auguste,</u> Mélanges de la Casa de Velazquez, vol. IX, 1973, 81-131, references to Emporion p. 106 and ff. and Fig. 8.

117. J. Guey, <u>Propos de numismatique statistique,</u> I, II, III, Bulletin de la Société Numismatique Française, 1967-68, 209-210, 270-273, 294-295.

118. The author does not intend to enter into discussion of the exact weight of the Roman pound, for this see M. Thirion, <u>Le trésor de Liberchies,</u> Bruxelles 1972, 49-53.

119. L. Villaronga, <u>Las marcas de valor en las monedas de Undicescen,</u> Congreso Aruqoelogico Nacional de Sevilla 1963, 331-338.

120. These marks, when the weight of the bronze coins of Emporion was reduced, became commonplace in its coinage, and were even copied by mints at Neronken, Saiti, etc.

121. L. Villaronga, see note 119.

122. <u>Crawf.</u> 596.

123. L. Villaronga, <u>El sistema metrologico semiuncial romano,</u> Numisma 120-131, 1973-74, 155-165.

124. L. Villaronga, <u>El hallazgo de Balsareny,</u> Numario Hispánico, X, 1961, 9-102.

125. J. Estrada and L. Villaronga, <u>La "Lauro" monetal y el hallazgo de Cànoves (Barcelona),</u> Ampurias XXIX, 1967, 135-194.

126. R. Martin Valls, <u>La circulación monetaria ibérica,</u> Valladolid 1967.

127. E. J. Haeberlin, <u>Die Münzen aus den Stadt Numantia des Lagern des Scipio un des Lagern bei Renieblas,</u> in A. Schulten, Numantia IV, München 1931, 234 and ff. M. Crawford, <u>Roman Republican Coin Hoards,</u> London 1969, no. 558. J. Romagosa, <u>Las monedas de los campamentos numantinos,</u> Acta Numismática II, 1972, 87-96.

128. M. Almagro, <u>Hallazgos monetarios emporitanos,</u> Ampurias IX-X, 1947-48, in Grupo de monedas del Cementerio Marti, primer grupa. 321. M. Crawford, no. 136, of the period 208-150 B.C.

129. Coin Hoards I, <u>The Royal Numismatic Society,</u> London 1975, 47, no. 155.

130. L. Villaronga, <u>Los tesoros de Azaila y la circulación monetaria en el Valle del Ebro,</u> printing.

131. J. M. de Navascues, <u>Las monedas hispánicas del Museo Arquelogico, National de Madrid,</u> II, Barcelona 1971.

132. M. Almagro, Las necrópolis de Ampurias, II, Barcelona 1955.

133. RIC I, 43.

134. L. Villaronga, La evolución epigráfica en las leyendas monetales ibéricas, Numisma, 8, 1958, 9-50.

135. E. Ripoll, J. M. Nuix and L. Villaronga, Las monedas partidas procedentes de las excavaciones de Emporion, Numisma 120-131, 1973-74, 75-90.

136. Crawf. 55.

137. Crawf. 77.

138. P. Galvez Izquierdo, Lépido en España, Zaragoza 1974.

139. E. Ripoll, J. M. Nuix and L. Villaronga, Consecuencias del estudio estadístico de las monedas halladas en las excavaciones de Emporion, given at the Methoden Kolloqium of the FMRD, of Frankfurt in Feb. 1976.

140. We refer to the classification of V.64.

PLATE I   SERIES 1

PLATE II   SERIES 2, 3

PLATE III SERIES 4, 5

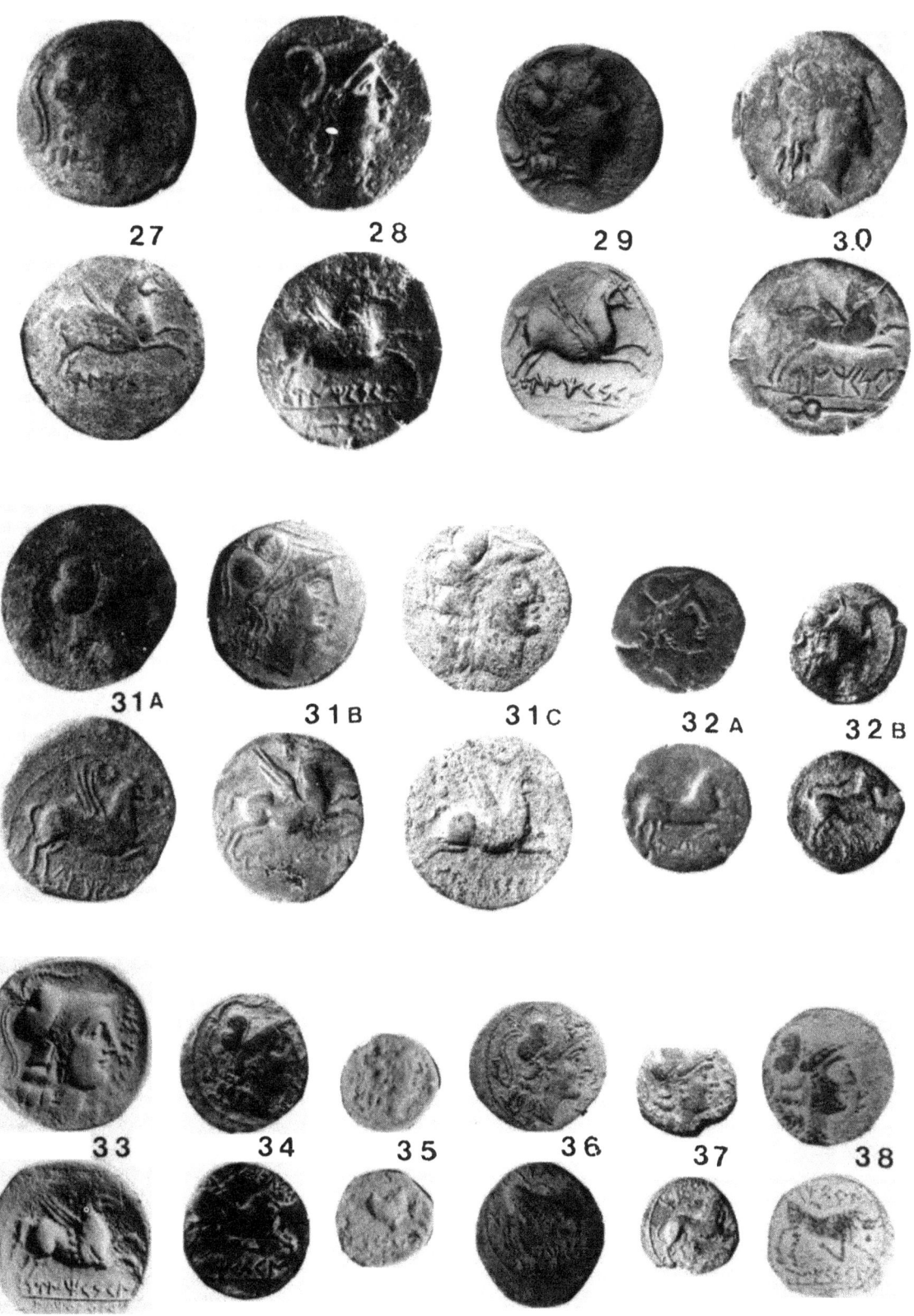

PLATE IV SERIES 6, 7

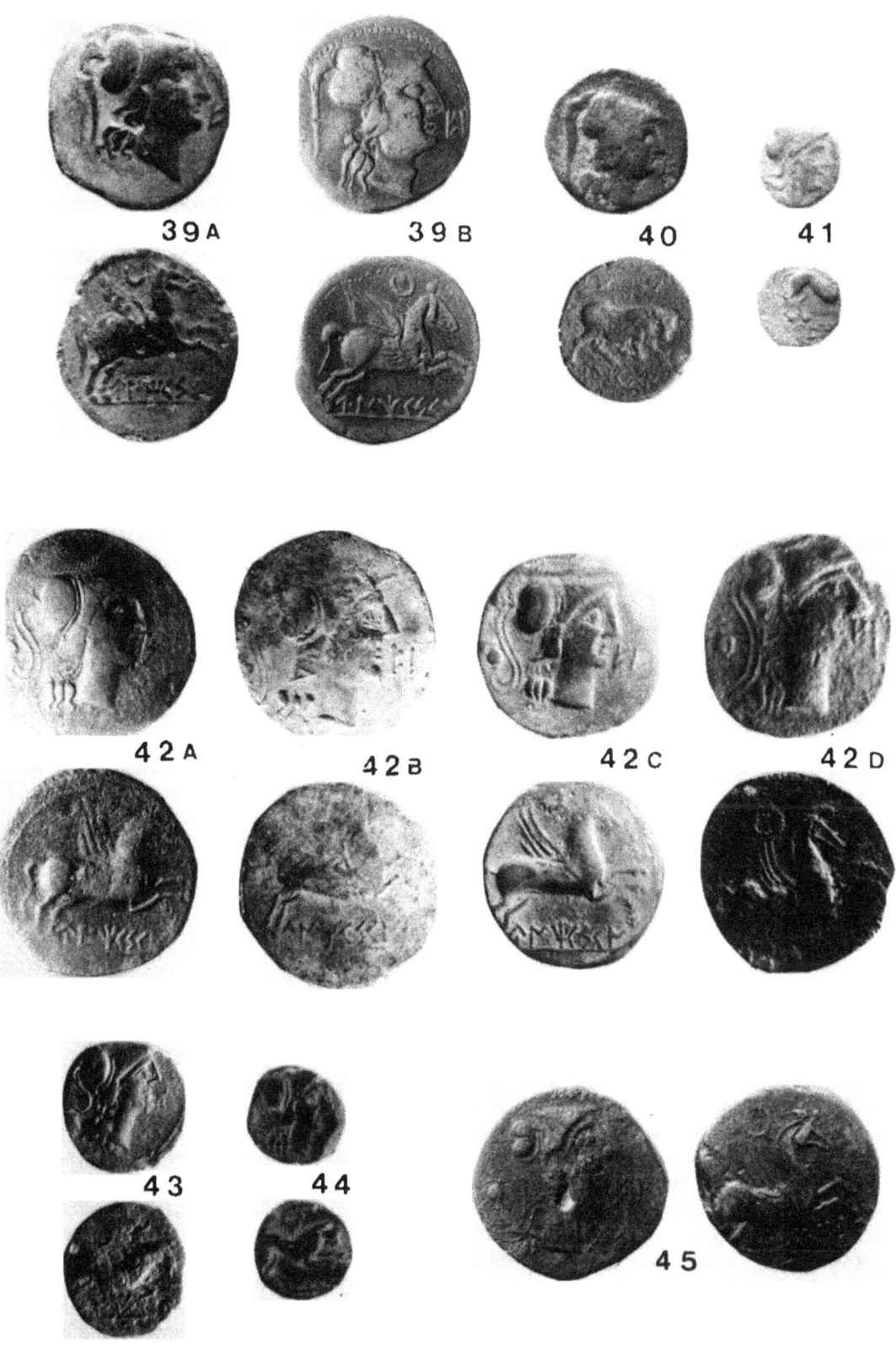

PLATE V SERIES 8, 9

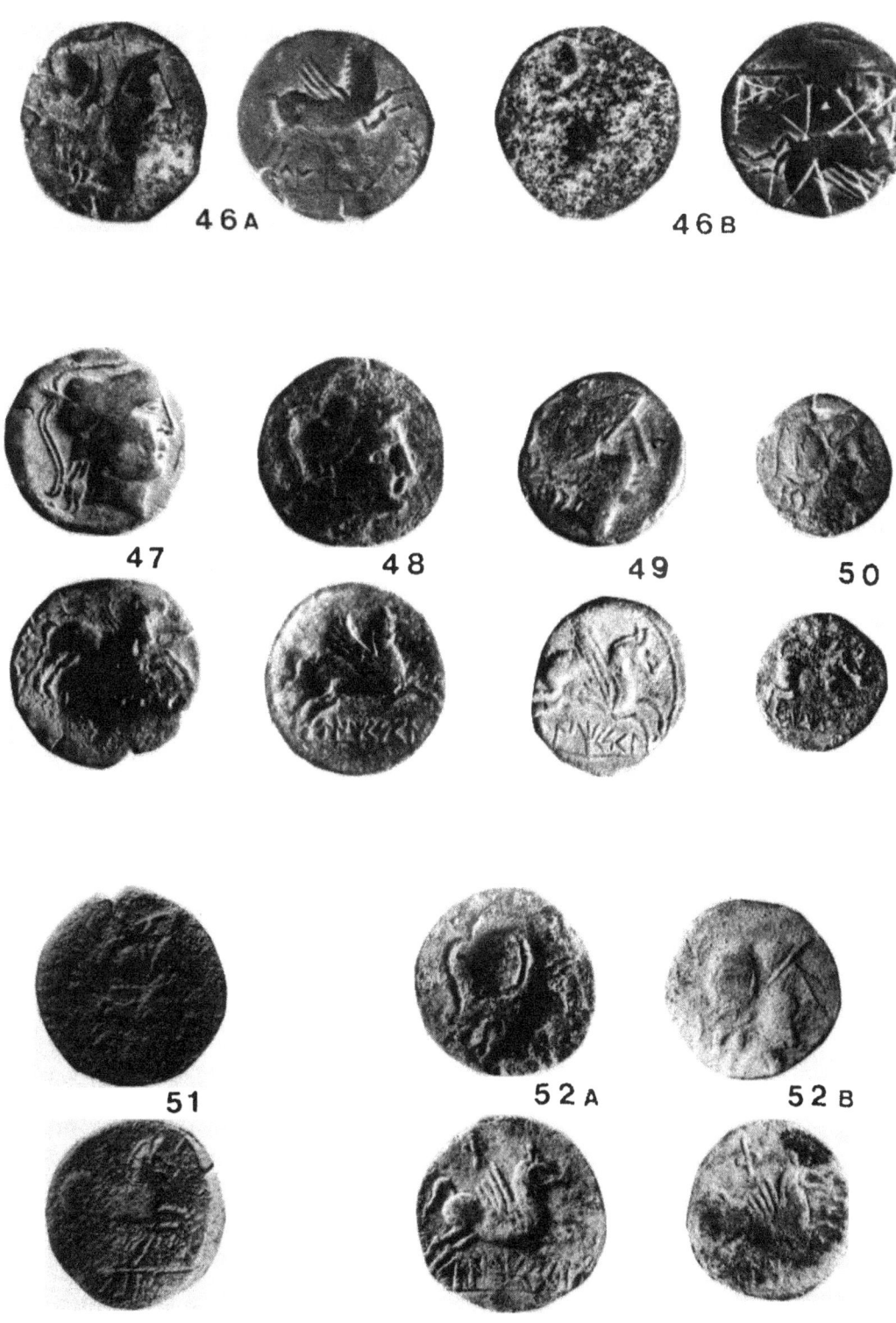

PLATE VI   SERIES 10, 11

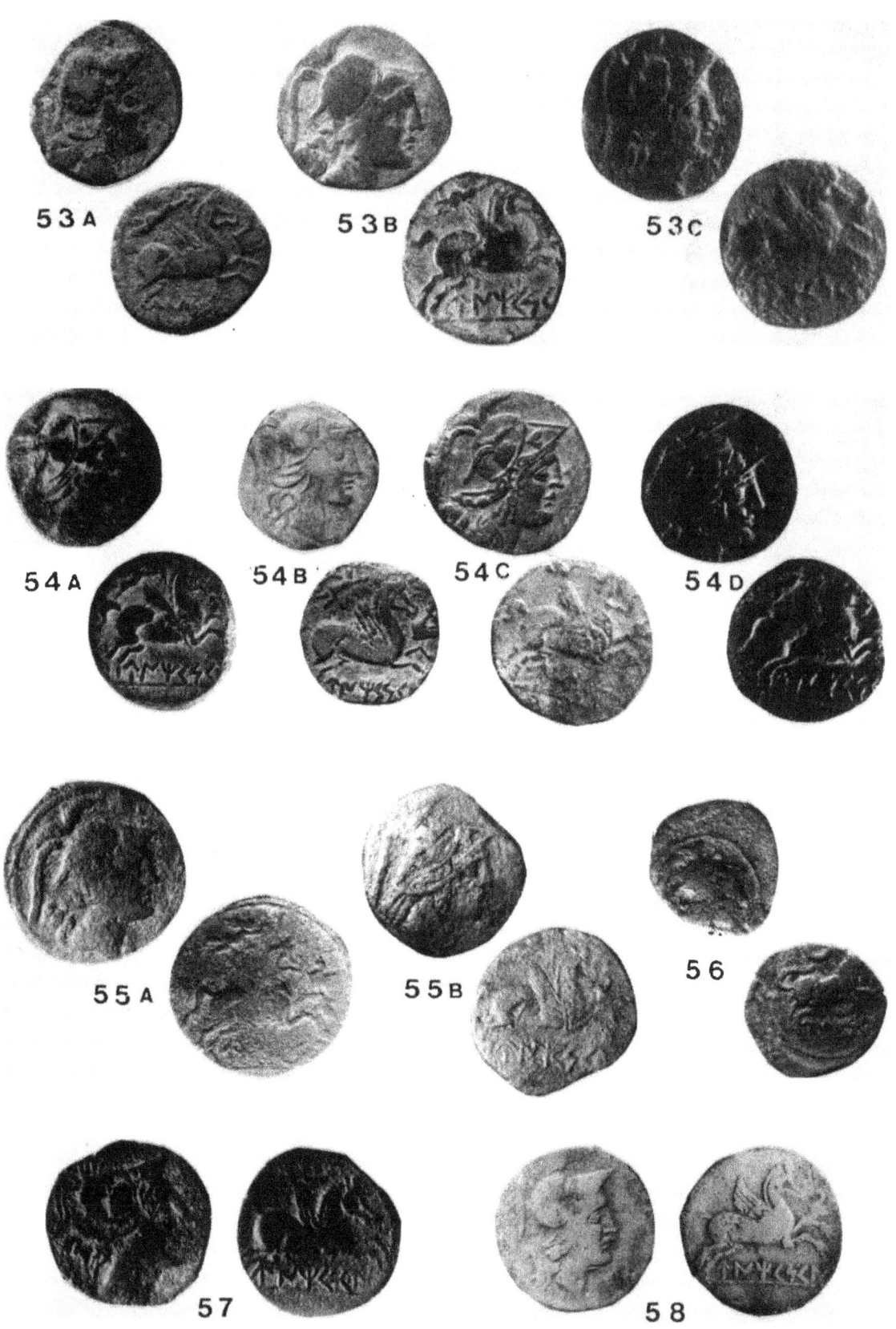

PLATE VII   SERIES 12

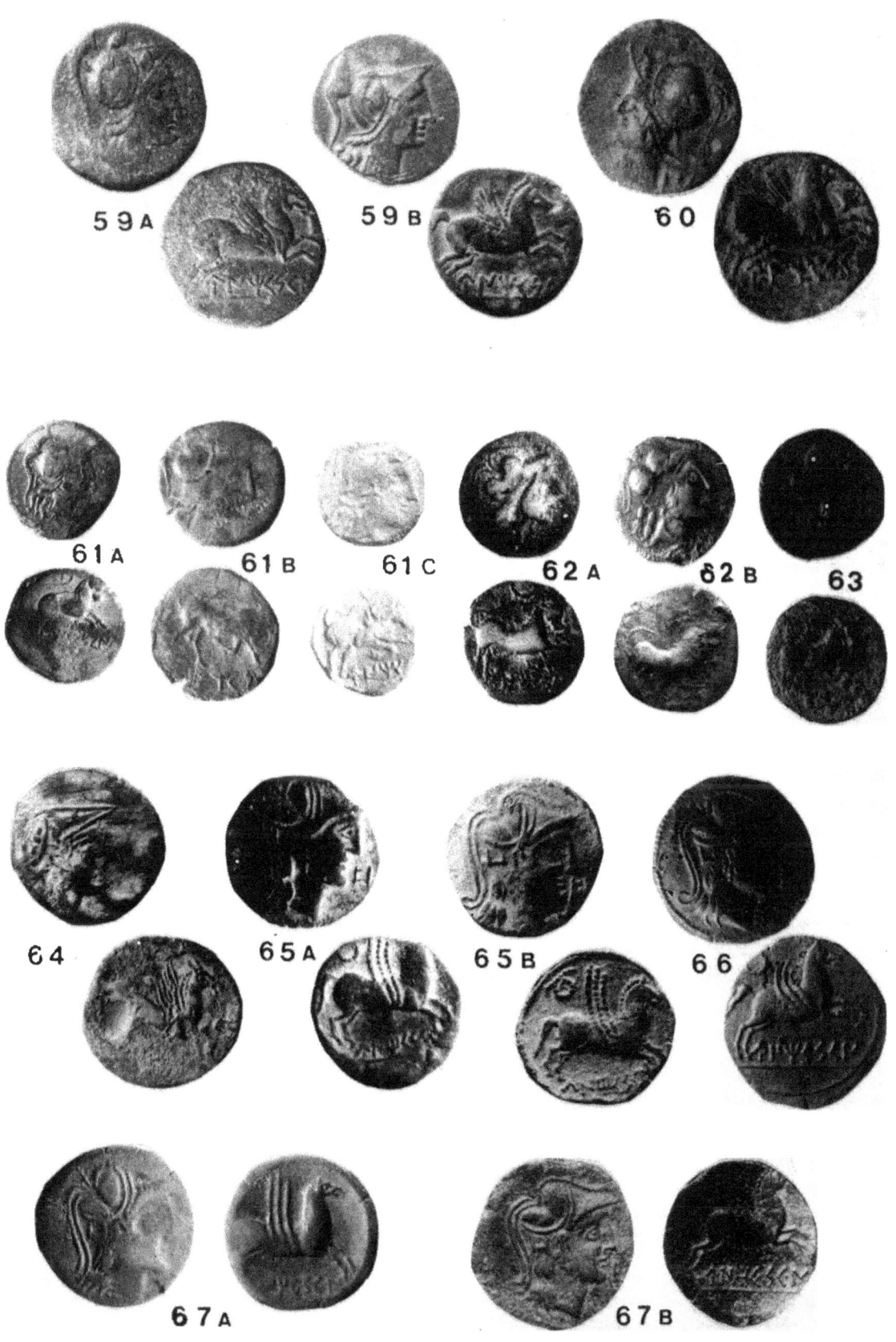

PLATE VIII   SERIES 13-16

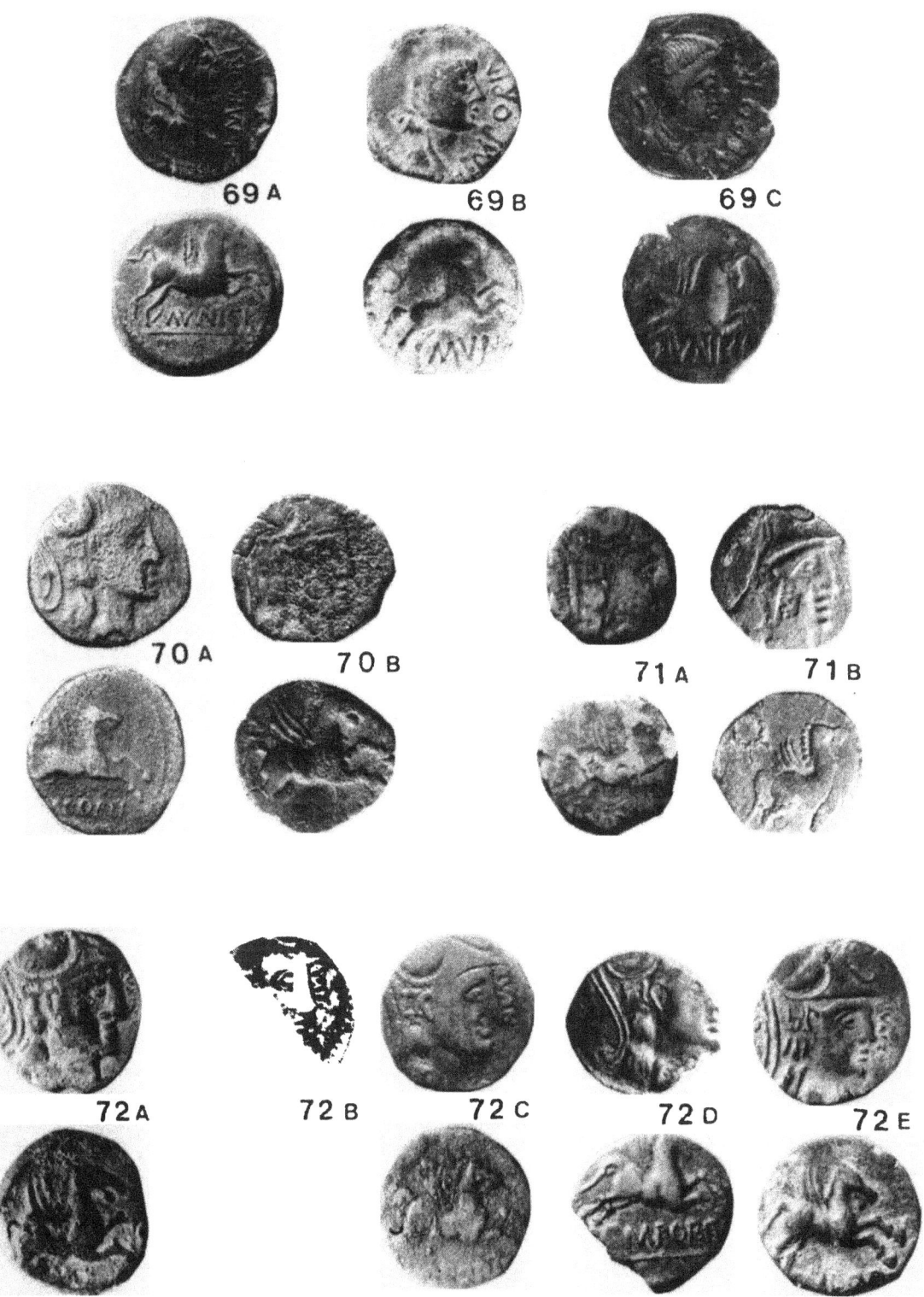

PLATE IX SERIES 17, 18

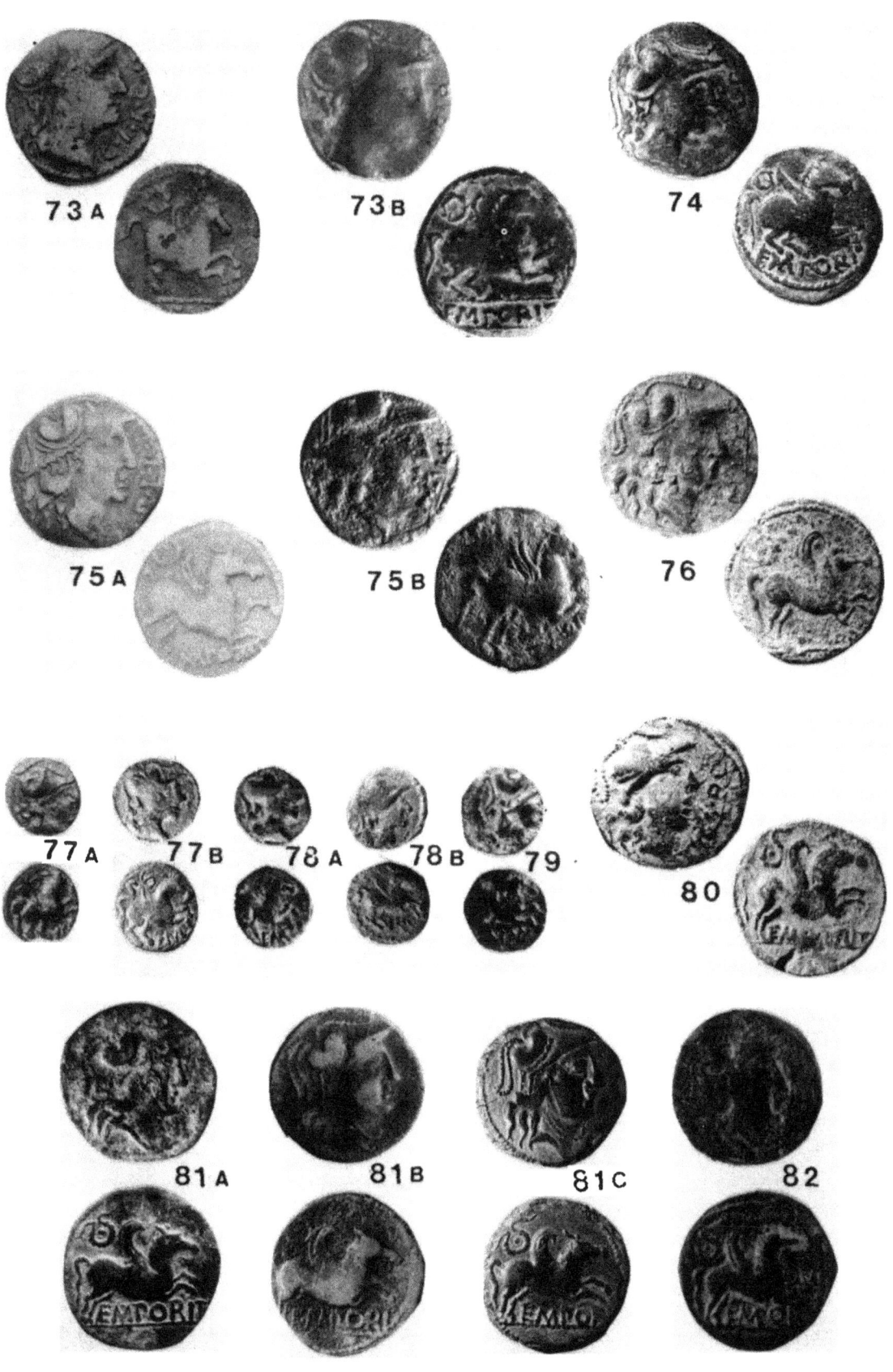

PLATE X   SERIES 19, 20

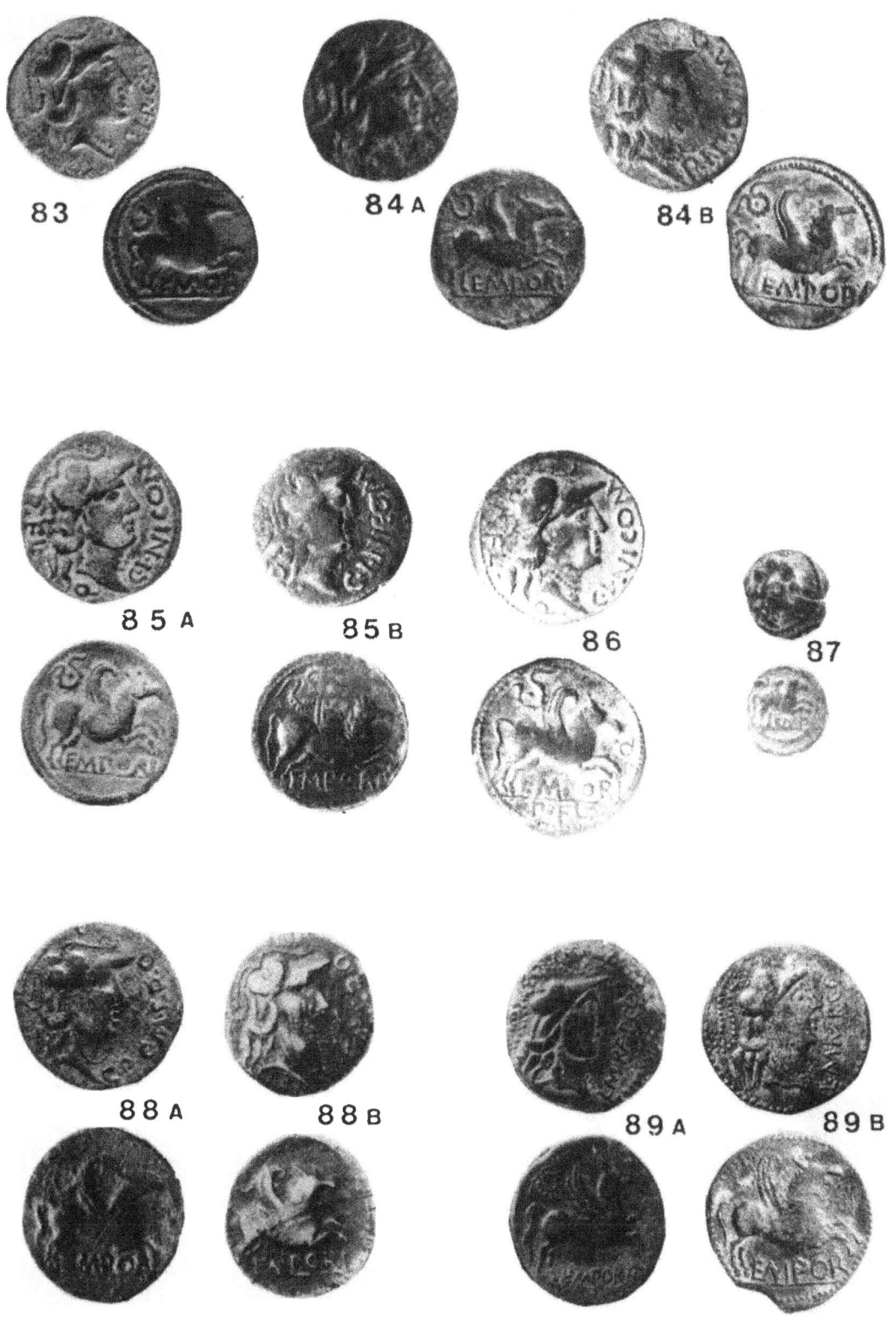

PLATE XI   SERIES 21, 22

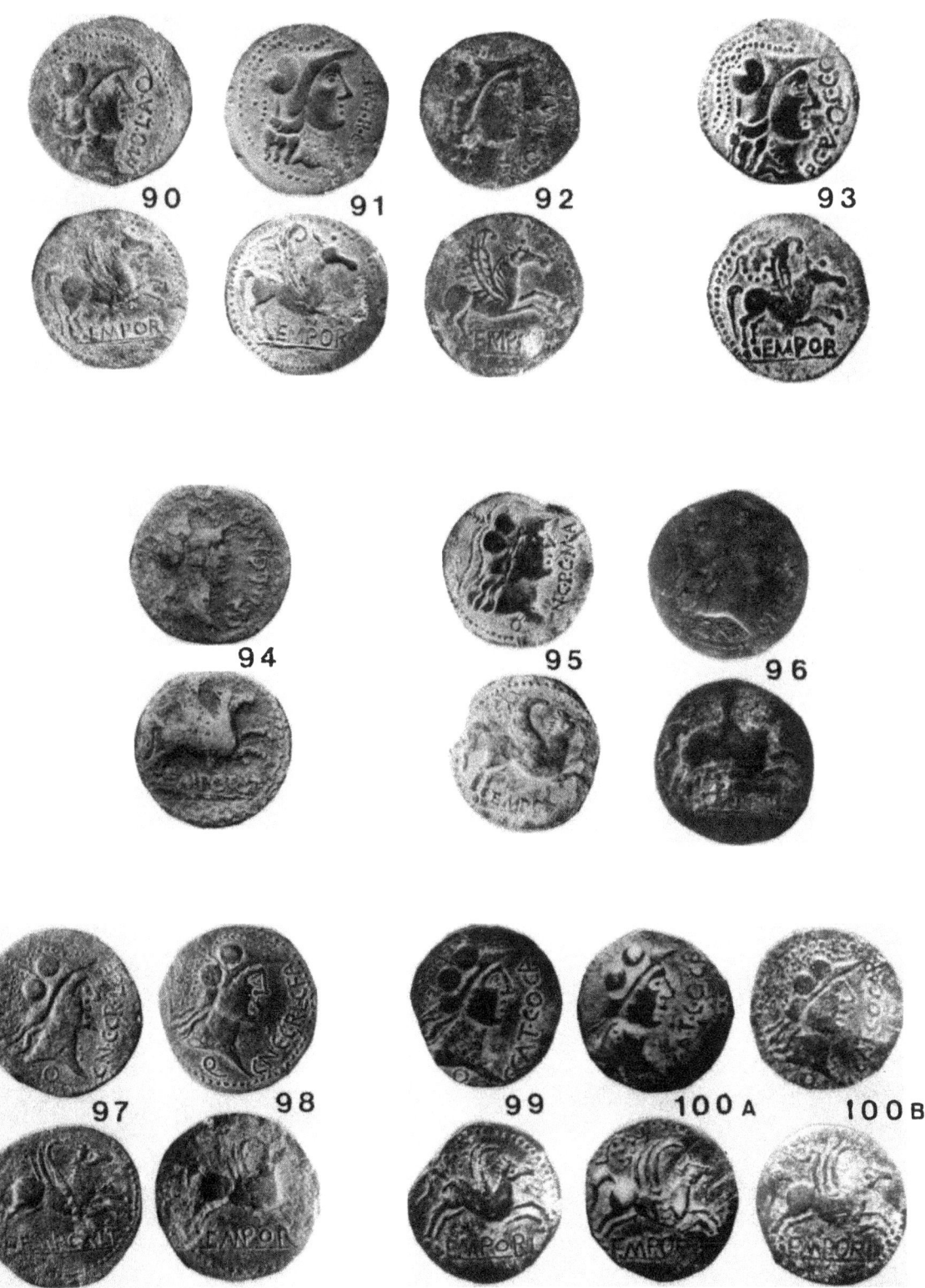

PLATE XII   SERIES 23, 24

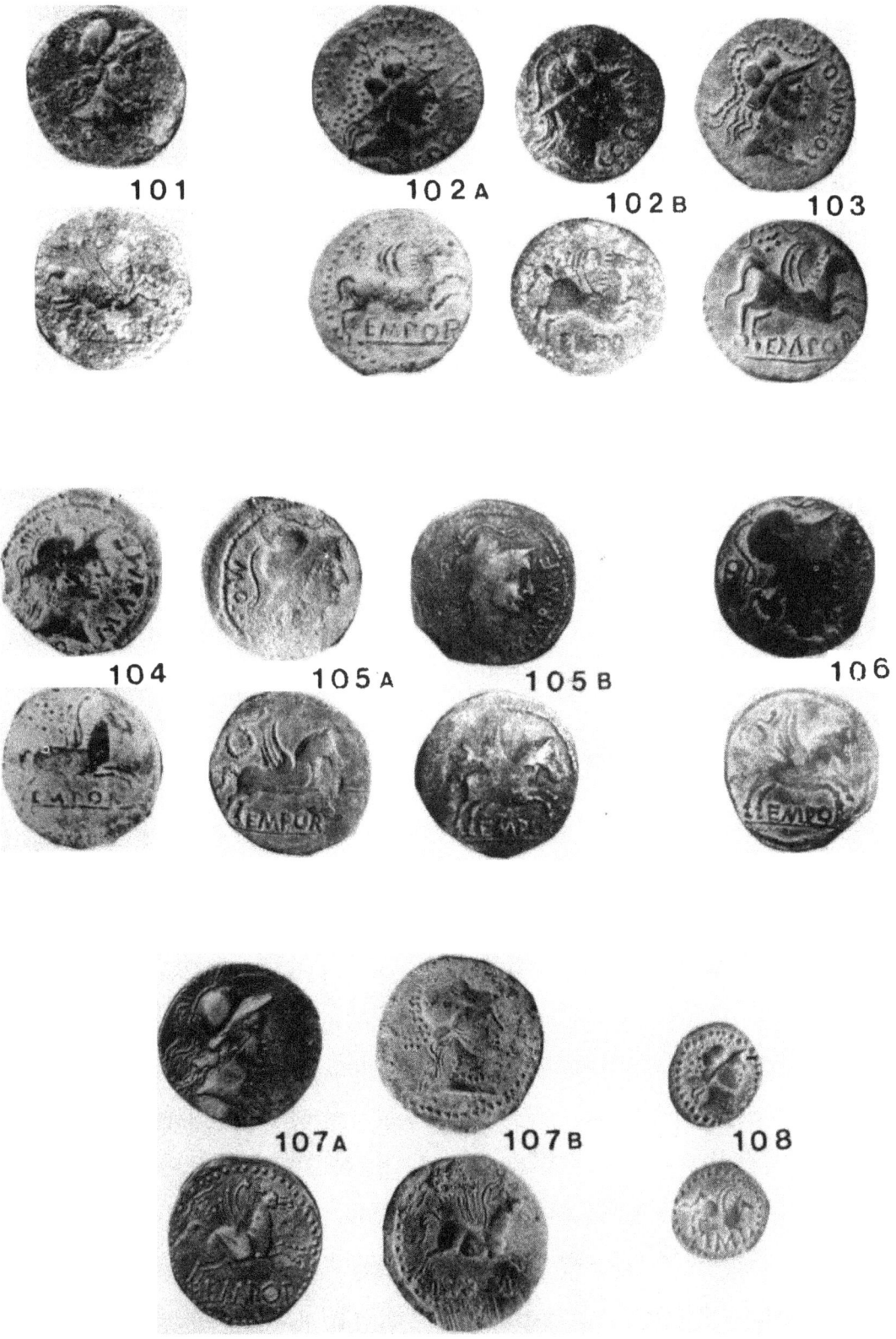

PLATE XIII   SERIES 24, 25

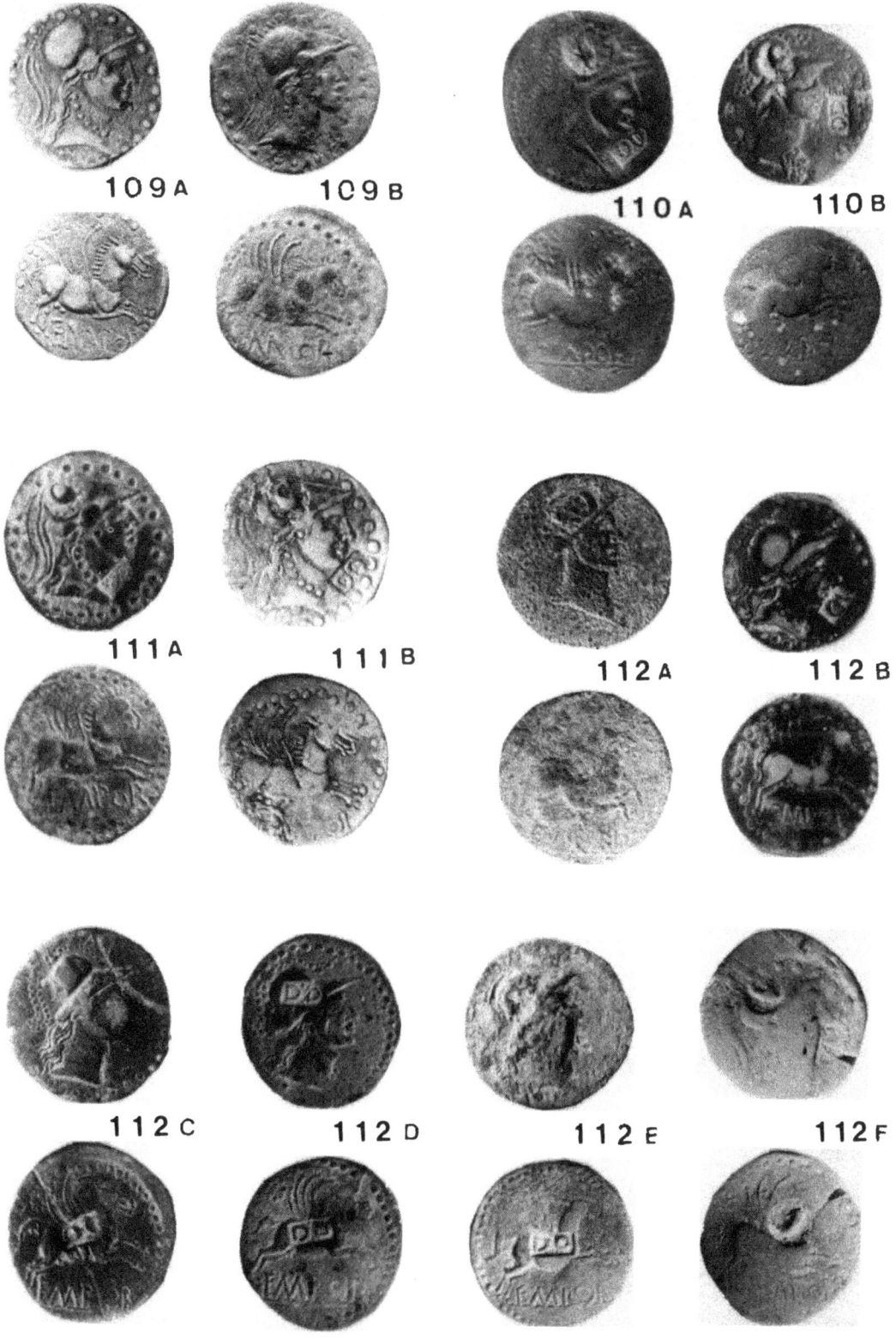

PLATE XIV   SERIES 25, 26

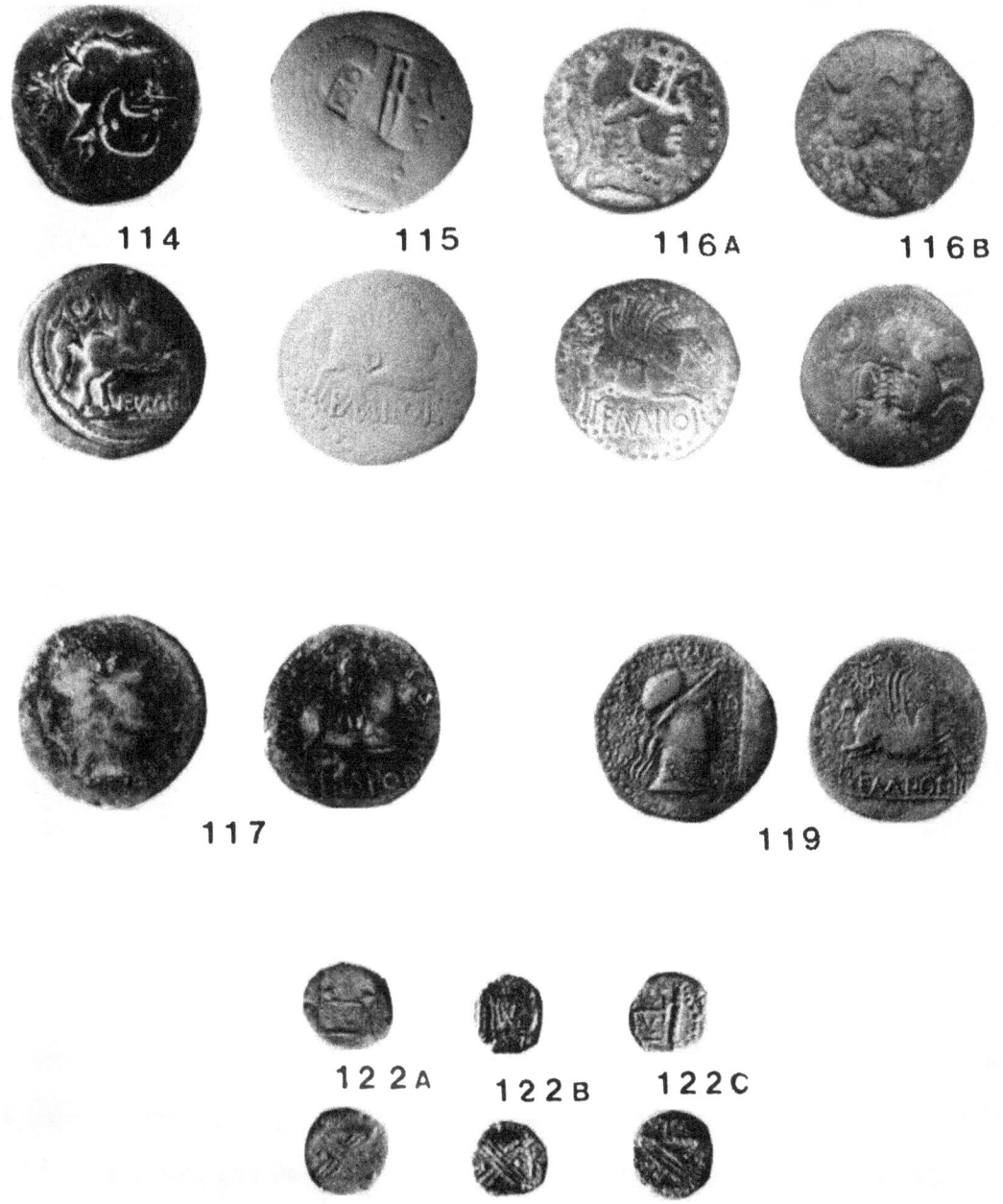

PLATE XV SERIES 27, 28

www.ingramcontent.com/pod-product-compliance
Lightning Source LLC
Chambersburg PA
CBHW050941010526
44108CB00060B/2875